Wharton Executive
EDUCATION ESSENTIALS

Finance & Accounting

Also Available

Wharton Executive Education Customer Centricity Essentials,
by Peter Fader

For more information,
visit *wdp.wharton.upenn.edu*

Wharton Executive
EDUCATION ESSENTIALS

Finance & Accounting

Richard A. Lambert

Wharton
DIGITAL PRESS
Philadelphia

Published by Wharton Digital Press
The Wharton School
University of Pennsylvania
3620 Locust Walk
2000 Steinberg Hall-Dietrich Hall
Philadelphia, PA 19104

Ebook ISBN: 978-1-61363-010-5
Paperback ISBN: 978-1-61363-009-9

Contents

Introduction

When Roger Enrico took over as CEO of PepsiCo, he reported mixed news in his first letter to shareholders in the 1996 Annual Report. On the one hand, PepsiCo as a whole reported record sales of $32 billion and record cash flow as well. On the other hand, profits weren't growing and not all of their segments were doing well. In fact, their beverage segment, the heart of their business, was doing poorly outside the United States, losing market share to archrival Coca-Cola. PepsiCo had invested billions of dollars in their restaurant segment (Pizza Hut, KFC, and Taco Bell) over the prior five years, yet the return they were achieving was disappointing.

After conducting a thorough analysis of its financial performance, Pepsi began making significant changes to its corporate strategy. They spun off their restaurants into a separate company, Tricon Global Restaurants (now called Yum! Brands) so they could concentrate on their snack and beverage segments. But they didn't stop with that change; the process of evaluating and revising strategy is an ongoing one. Shortly thereafter, they acquired Tropicana and Quaker Oats (who also owned Gatorade). They have continued to make changes to their segments and product lines, and as recently as 2010, they reacquired control of two of their largest bottlers. By 2010, through this series of strategic shifts, PepsiCo's revenue had skyrocketed to nearly $60 billion. Their earnings and their stock price performance have both substantially outperformed the S&P 500 over the period from 1997 to 2010.

These are major corporate-level changes, but the same principles apply at all levels of the organization. Managers must constantly evaluate their firms' strategies to assess how their decisions have been performing, to modify these strategies as conditions change, and to devise new strategies to boost performance in the future. Which activities should we devote more resources to and which should we cut back on? Which resources are not being used effectively? Should we outsource an activity or continue to perform it ourselves? Business decisions like these need to be based on information, and financial statements are a major source of this information.

But many managers don't have a background in accounting and finance, so they don't have the tools they need to answer these questions. They don't understand the reports they are given to help them make these decisions. They either ignore the information completely, they misinterpret what the numbers mean, or they aren't even aware of what isn't in the numbers at all. All of these behaviors are dangerous to your firm's financial health. They are like trying to fly a plane with no instruments and with the windshield fogged up. The goal of *Wharton Executive Education Finance & Accounting Essentials* isn't to teach readers how to compile the financials. Leave that to the accounting and finance staffs, the CPAs, and the CFOs; they know all the rules and regulations. Instead, my goal is to teach you how to use and interpret the data they give you. Whether you are an experienced manager, executive, or leader at a public company or private business, regardless of size, mastering financial statements can help you make better decisions and make you more valuable to your firm.

Although accounting statements are filled with numbers, in many ways, accounting is more like a language. Accounting rules provide the mechanism by which business transactions and economic events get translated into numbers. What do the words attached to the numbers mean? Like every field, finance and accounting have their own jargon, and an important part of being able to understand and communicate is learning this vocabulary or language. Income is different from cash. Depreciation doesn't mean how much an asset's economic value has gone down. Liabilities can be good things. Too much cash can be bad. GAAP, NPV, ROA, EBITDA, WACC, leverage . . . What do these terms mean?

Many people are also surprised to learn that financial statements carry a large degree of ambiguity and subjectivity. Just as English majors argue about the interpretation of a soliloquy in *Hamlet*, managers and accountants can disagree regarding the best measure of a company's performance or financial status. The reason for this subjectivity is that accounting statements have to be put together while much is still in process. Although we could eliminate this ambiguity if we waited until the end of the firm's life before we tallied up its profits, this information would be too late to help with decisions that have to be made while the firm is still operating.

To provide more timely and useful information, accounting statements do not just look backward and tell you what happened in the past; virtually every number on a balance sheet or income statement is based in part on estimates of what will happen in the future. Unfortunately, future cash flows and events are never known for sure. This is what opens the door for manipulation by unscrupulous management. Even well-meaning managers are often overly optimistic about their firm's future prospects. To deal with these potential problems, restrictions are placed on what kind of information about the future is permitted to be transmitted through the financial statements. Auditors and other checks and balances exist to limit management's ability to misrepresent the firm's performance, but these elements don't work perfectly because they don't have a crystal ball into the future either. In this book, you will learn how this subjectivity and judgment affects the numbers and about what aspects of the future are incorporated and what others aren't. This will help you learn to read between the lines of financial statements and know when to be skeptical.

Once you better understand accounting and finance, you will also begin to see that the numbers that your firm supplies to external parties (like shareholders or tax authorities) aren't the numbers you want to use to run your firm—and no, the reason doesn't have anything to do with cheating or misrepresentation. At a minimum, you will want more detail about the performance of the individual parts of your company than annual reports and tax returns can provide. In addition, you want data that help you predict how costs and revenues will change if you make different decisions. External reporting systems typically sort items only by their type (for example, production costs are separate from marketing costs), but you would like information within each category to help you understand how your costs behave: what costs are fixed versus variable, what costs are sunk or committed to, what costs are direct versus allocated, and so on.

Finally, the reports provided to external parties like shareholders and creditors are compiled using rules that are regulated by standard-setting bodies.[1] Given that the company already has to compile numbers in a particular way to satisfy these external regulatory demands, many companies choose to use these exact same numbers for internal decision-making purposes also (because it's cheaper than coming up with an additional reporting system). Be careful. These rules are often designed for simplicity, to be conservative, or to achieve other objectives—not to measure your performance or financial position as accurately as possible. I will discuss some of these problems and how they can distort your performance measures.

Another important reason for managers to learn accounting and finance skills is to help them become more valuable participants in discussions of corporate strategy and to be more effective in championing their own ideas. Ultimately, an important part of these decisions is based on what they will do to "the numbers." Many investment proposals involve spending money now on something that will (hopefully) yield benefits in the future. Therefore, investment decisions are based on predictions about the future and on how these predictions will manifest in term of future cash flows and profits.

Here it is vital to understand what accounting and finance skills can do and what they can't do. Accounting and finance skills can't tell you whether an investment in a proposed research and development plan will yield a drug that the FDA will approve. Accounting and finance can't tell you whether consumers will like the new product you're thinking of introducing (like New Coke). Accounting and finance can't tell you whether an acquisition whose success requires blending two completely different corporate cultures (like AOL and Time Warner) will work. Experience and gut instincts are invaluable skills to managers in trying to make these judgments.

What accounting and finance skills can tell you is how big the probability of success needs to be and how big the benefits need to be if things work out in order for the investment to be worth the costs. More generally, accounting and finance provide an economic framework for comparing alternative strategies for how to invest your money in terms of how much value they add to the company. They can help you assess what an acceptable rate of return is. They can tell you how it depends on the riskiness of the strategy. They can tell you how much more a strategy that won't pay off for many years has to earn compared to an investment that generates its return more quickly.

Moreover, by forcing you to tie your forecasts of future events into income statements, balance sheets, and cash flow statements, the framework of accounting and finance adds discipline to the process. Often managerial projections are fueled more by ego or hope than by reality. Accounting and finance techniques give you an opportunity to assess the reasonableness of the assumptions underlying the predictions and the sensitivity of the predicted results to changes in the assumptions. By forcing you to construct projected income statements, balance sheets, and cash flow statements that are internally consistent, these skills also reduce the risk of leaving something significant out of the analysis completely.

In this book, I will explain:

- The role of balance sheets, income statements, and cash flow statements.
- How these financial statements relate to one another.
- Financial reporting concepts, such as revenue recognition, inventory costing, depreciation, and taxes.
- How to dissect an income statement and balance sheet to understand the drivers of profitability.
- How your capital structure—the mix of debt and equity you use to finance your assets—influences your profits and your risk.
- How you can identify and estimate the relevant costs for decisions.
- How to evaluate investment strategies and conduct discounted cash flow analysis.
- How to put all of this together to develop a coherent business strategy.

Finances affect every aspect of business. Once executives and managers understand the rudiments of financial statements and the tools of financial analysis, managers can understand what is driving revenue, pinpoint where the organization is doing well, and analyze why performance isn't living up to expectations. Gaining a better grasp of financials helps managers know what questions to ask and what to focus on, determine what's most important, and know what to avoid and what to pay attention to. Fueled by better understanding of the drivers of performance, leaders can make better strategic decisions, make changes in the business, and better gauge what to acquire or sell. It's the synergies that arise from merging managerial experience with finance and accounting skills that can generate the most value to you and to your organization. Hence, boosting your own financial knowledge makes good business sense.

Chapter 1

Your Company's Financial Health and Performance: What Financial Statements Can Tell You

In this chapter:

- The 3 fundamental financial statements
- How the 3 financial statements relate

When Krispy Kreme went public in 2000, it was hard to resist its sugary doughnuts or its stock. America is well known for having a sweet tooth, and investors figured consumers would keep buying those sugary sweets the way they kept digesting Big Macs. By the summer of 2003, the stock had skyrocketed to $50, more than double its initial offering price. By the end of 2003, Krispy Kreme had opened 357 outlets, including some stores overseas. Revenues rose from $300 million in 2000 to $649 million in 2003. But by the summer of 2004, a slew of low-carbohydrate diets were in vogue that made doughnuts a no-no. America's tastes had changed, and those doughnuts and its stock began to turn stale.

Krispy Kreme's aggressive expansion was funded in part by sharply increasing their debt load; long-term debt rose from a modest $3.5 million at the end of 2000 to $56 million in 2002 to $137 million in 2003. Accordingly, interest costs rose sharply. As revenues started to drop, profits declined even more sharply. By 2005, the stock had slid to $6, and the company started closing stores. Revenues in 2010 were only $362 million, compared to

$649 million in its heyday in 2003. However, their stock price bounced back slightly in 2011.

Understanding Krispy Kreme's opportunities and risks as it grew demanded reading and understanding its income statement, cash flow statement, and balance sheet. In this chapter, we'll discuss the importance of each of those financial statements and cover the following topics:

- How the balance sheet represents a snapshot of the company's resources (assets) at a fixed period of time and also provides information about the firm's capital structure and its riskiness.
- Income statements, which measure a company's revenues, expenses, and profitability.
- Cash flow statements, which provide information about liquidity and the sources and uses of cash, the lifeblood of the company.
- How income statements and cash flow statements differ.

The 3 Fundamental Financial Statements

The financial statements—the balance sheet, income statement, and cash flow statement—are an important means by which timely information is provided to managers as well as to investors, creditors, and other users of financial statements. Each statement furnishes a different type of information. Each is useful in its own right; however, understanding how the three are linked is vital to assessing a company's strengths and weaknesses. Together they provide a fuller picture of a company's current financial status and offer a glimpse into its future. In this chapter, we will describe what each statement does and how they are interrelated. An example of a set of financial statements is contained in chapter 2.

What distinguishes the three statements? The balance sheet lists the resources (assets) the firm has acquired and still retains, as well as the nature of the claims on these assets (liabilities and owners' equity). The balance sheet is analogous to a snapshot; it represents the financial position of the firm at a specific point in time (for example, at the end of the quarter or year). Income statements report the profitability of the firm during the period. Cash flow statements provide information about the inflows and outflows of cash during the period. These latter two statements therefore help provide information about how and why the firm's financial status has changed since the end of the prior period. Profitability (value generated) and liquidity (cash generated) are not the same thing, however, which is why we have two different statements.

Balance Sheet

The phrase "balance sheet" comes from a relation that financial statements must always preserve:

Assets = Liabilities + Owners' Equity

This equation simply states that the assets or resources of the firm have to be claimed by someone. If it is not someone else (the liability holders or creditors), then it is the owners. A simple example from personal finance illustrates: if you have a house that's worth $500,000 and have a mortgage with a balance of $300,000, your owners' equity in the house is the difference, $200,000. Although the concept might look simple, we will see that this relationship has important implications for understanding how to interpret financial statements and also for understanding how balance sheets and income statements are related. The fact that balance sheets always balance to the penny is one of the factors that contributes to the illusion of exactness in accounting. A balance sheet that balances does not mean there are no errors, and it does not mean that everything is valued correctly. If we misvalued our house at, say, $700,000, we would similarly mismeasure the value of our equity at $400,000. Everything still balances, but the economic picture presented is distorted relative to reality.

Assets

A company's balance sheet starts with its assets. Assets are the keys to sustaining the company. Assets represent the resources a company has available to use to generate profits or provide other future economic benefits, such as the ability to pay back debt. Assets include the following types of resources:

- Financial assets: cash, notes and accounts receivable, marketable securities, derivative instruments.
- Physical assets: inventories, plant and equipment, real estate.
- Intangible assets: patents and copyrights, other contractual rights, goodwill.

Assets are grouped on the balance sheet into two categories, current and noncurrent. Current assets are those expected to generate their benefits within one year; examples include cash, accounts receivable, inventories, and many types of marketable securities. Noncurrent assets are expected to take longer than a year and include property plant and equipment, long-term investments, and most intangibles.

Valuing Assets

All of the assets, liabilities, and owners' equity accounts are expressed in dollars. How do we place a value on them? Accountants have traditionally used historical cost for most assets. The historical cost is the amount that was paid for the asset when it was acquired. The virtue of historical cost accounting is that the numbers are objective and reliably measured. Unfortunately, historical costs can become out-of-date and lose their relevance over time.

To address this problem, an alternative basis for valuing assets termed "fair value" was developed. If you have heard the phrase "mark to market," this is what fair value tries to do—to estimate what the current market value of the asset is. Unfortunately, this is often not easy to do with any precision, which leads to questions about the reliability of these values. The virtue of fair-value accounting is that values are more up-to-date, so they are, in principle, more relevant to decision making. The "relevance versus reliability" debate regarding which valuation method is better has gone on for many decades, and it will continue far into the future. When an asset is newly acquired, its historical cost and market value are usually the same thing. It is only after the asset is acquired that the two values diverge.

For financial assets, obtaining reliable values is often easier to do because there are actively traded markets for many of them (e.g., the stock market and bond market).[2] Financial assets (and an increasing number of financial liabilities) are therefore shown on the balance sheet at their fair value. But for many physical assets (especially property plant and equipment) and intangible assets, assets are so unique and markets so inactive that market values are deemed too unreliable to use. Accountants use historical costs (sometimes adjusted downward to reflect depreciation) for them.

When accountants provide inaccurate values, this can cause users of the financial statements to make poor decisions regarding what to do with the assets. Although both overvaluation errors and undervaluation errors have consequences, a long-held view in accounting (and by the courts) is that overvaluation is the more serious problem. That is, if we tell you an asset is worth $100 and it turns out to be worth only $80, that is a more serious error than if we tell you it's worth $80 and it turns out to generate $100 of benefits. Because "bad surprises" have more serious consequences than "good surprises," accounting statements are influenced by a policy of conservatism. In particular, many nonfinancial assets are valued on the financial statements at neither their historical cost nor their current market value, but instead at the lower of the two. The "lower of cost or market" method recognizes declines in asset values (called impairments) but not increases in asset values.

To be recognized by accountants, the value of the asset must be measurable with a reasonable degree of precision. Because of this requirement, many assets that are important from an economic perspective but are considered difficult to value are often excluded. Brand names are a prime example. For example, Coca-Cola is considered to be one of the most valuable brands in the world, and certainly one of the most valuable assets that Coca-Cola possesses, yet it does not appear on their balance sheet.[3] To make things even more confusing to new readers of financial statements, that same brand name would be recognized if it were obtained via a corporate acquisition. In this case, there is an objective, defined transaction that can be referred to as a means of establishing the value of a brand name. Brands and other types of intangible assets that have been developed internally lack such an objective valuation and therefore do not appear on the balance sheet.[4]

For all of these reasons, one has to be careful when looking at asset values on a balance sheet. When we sum up the asset values to calculate total assets, for example, we could be adding our cash in the bank to the price we paid for a building 20 years ago to the current market value of marketable securities we hold. It is not clear what, if anything, this sum means economically. It is certainly not the current value of the firm's assets. If you were to try to use this asset value in the calculation of a performance measure like return on assets (ROA), you would need to understand that your measure is distorted by the accounting valuation problems. Understanding what is included and excluded from financial statements and how things are valued are critical skills to effectively analyze them.

Liabilities

Liabilities are obligations of the firm to transfer assets or provide services to other entities in the future as a result of past transactions or events. These are claims by creditors against the assets of the firm. Liabilities include the following types of obligations:

- Obligations to transfer assets: notes and accounts payable, taxes payable, bonds payable.
- Obligations to provide services: rents and royalties received in advance, warranty liabilities, frequent-flier miles.

Like assets, liabilities are classified as current if they are due within a year and noncurrent if they are due more than a year from now. Short-term liabilities are simply valued at the amount to be repaid or the estimated cost of providing the service. However, if the time period until the obligation becomes due is long (more than a year), the present value of the cash payments to be made is used. We will discuss present-value calculations in chapter 6.

Some liabilities, such as accounts payable, are easy to value because the liability specifies a dollar amount to be paid and a date when it is due. Other liabilities, such as warranties, require more judgment to decide what the cost of fulfilling this obligation will be. Pension obligations and postretirement health-care benefits pose especially difficult challenges in valuation because estimates must be made of highly uncertain events such as employee turnover and mortality, and about future interest rates, wage increases, and/or health-care cost inflation trends. Like assets, a company can have significant obligations that do not show up on its balance sheet. In fact, many companies expend significant resources engaging in what is known as "off-balance-sheet financing." This is intended to make the balance sheet project a rosier picture of the company's health than is actually accurate.

Owners' Equity

Owners' equity is the residual interest in the assets of an entity that remains after deducting its liabilities. This is sometimes called the "net assets" or "net worth" of the firm. It comes from the following sources:

- Contributed capital: amounts the company obtains by selling shares. This is sometimes called common stock or additional paid in capital.
- Retained earnings: the profits of the firm (these belong to the owners) that have been reinvested back into the firm.

Contributed capital accounts are valued at the market value that existed at the time shares were issued or repurchased. Retained earnings are valued by adding the income for the period minus the dividends paid out during the period to the beginning balance of retained earnings. Note that the owners' equity on the firm's balance sheet is not the same as the market value of the firm's shares. This follows directly from the fact that some assets are not included on the balance sheet or are not valued at their market value. The same is true for the liabilities listed on the balance sheet. Therefore, the difference between assets and liabilities will not be the market value of the owner's equity.

What to Look For on the Balance Sheet

In examining a balance sheet, we're trying to critically assess the resources the company has. Are they sufficient to support the level of operations the company expects to be operating at? If not, then the company will have to make substantial new investments. Do they have the money to do that, and if not, how will they obtain it? At the other extreme, do they have more assets than they need, and should they be scaling back or finding ways to use them more efficiently?

It is also useful to look at the composition, not just the overall scale, of the assets. The best way to do this is to construct what's called a "common-size" balance sheet. We do this by dividing each item on the balance sheet by total assets. This gives us the percentage of total assets that are cash, the percent that are receivables, and so on. The rescaled assets will sum to 1.0 (or to 100%). If receivables are unusually high, is this a sign we're having trouble collecting from customers? If inventories are high, is this a sign we're having trouble selling our product, or is it instead an indicator we are preparing for future growth in sales? If we've made a lot of acquisitions, goodwill is likely to be high.[5] Do we really expect to obtain future benefits from this asset, or does it simply reflect the amount we've overpaid to acquire other firms?

On a common-size balance sheet, the other side of the balance sheet also sums to 1.0 (because Assets = Liabilities + Owners' Equity). This gives us an easy-to-interpret indication of how our assets have been financed. What percentage of our assets are financed by equity and what percentage are financed by debt? As we will see in chapter 4, this is an important indicator of the riskiness of the firm. We can also see what percentage of our debt is short-term versus long-term. This is helpful in formulating cash management strategies to repay the debt. Do we have enough current assets to cover our current liabilities (with some margin of safety)? If not, we'll need to have contingency plans in place in case we run short of cash.

For example, Table 1.1 illustrates how Krispy Kreme's assets grew in the years following its initial public offering (IPO) and how their mix of financing evolved.

Table 1.1
Krispy Kreme's asset, liabilities, and owners' equity accounts after going public
(numbers in thousands)

	2000	2001	2002	2003	2004	...	2010
Long-Term Debt	$3,505	$4,643	$55,564	$137,114	$90,950	...	$32,874
Total Liabilities	$52,663	$76,131	$148,180	$220,194	$239,335	...	$93,498
Total Shareholders' Equity	$122,387	$182,210	$265,439	$436,409	$240,943	...	$76,428
Total Assets	$175,050	$258,341	$413,619	$656,603	$480,278	...	$169,926

As we see, the assets grew enormously over the period between 2000 and 2003, consistent with Krispy Kreme's rapid expansion in terms of number of stores. Long-term debt became an increasingly large percentage of the total mix of financing, peaking at 21% of total assets in 2003. Beginning in 2004, we see that assets began to drop as Krispy Kreme began to discontinue operations in many places. In the last column, we see that Krispy Kreme is a substantially smaller company than in its heyday of the early 2000s. A substantial portion of their assets are still financed by liabilities and long-term debt.

Income Statement

The income statement, sometimes called the statement of earnings, is often the statement that people pay the most attention to because it measures what owners care most directly about: making profits. The format starts with revenues (the inflows from selling goods and services) and then subtracts expenses (the outflows needed to be able to produce those goods and services).

For Krispy Kreme, their revenues and net income figures following their IPO were as follows:

Table 1.2
Krispy Kreme's revenues and net income after going public
(numbers in thousands)

	2000	2001	2002	2003	2004	...	2010
Revenues	$300,729	$394,241	$490,728	$649,345	$707,766	...	$361,955
Net Income	$13,782	$24,213	$31,058	$48,563	$(198,339)	...	$7,599

In Table 1.2, we see that during the period from 2000 to 2003, revenues more than doubled and profits almost quadrupled. Revenues continued to grow in 2004 because of the rapid expansion of stores in the past, but the profitability of the stores had halted and Krispy Kreme reported losses bigger than the sum of all their profits since the IPO. In the last column, consistent with the asset numbers in the first table, Krispy Kreme's revenue numbers are back to the level they were when they first went public, and in 2010, they reported positive income for the first time since 2003.

Ideally, the income statement would show the increase in economic value the firm has been able to generate for its shareholders during the period. This is a very different thing than reporting the increase or decrease in cash during the period. Many value-increasing activities do not give rise to cash in the same period. For example, we could generate the same value for the firm via a sales contract in which we got paid now or via one in which we got paid (more) in the future. In fact, there are an infinite number of combinations of streams of future cash flow that have the exact same economic value. Accounting income looks more broadly at the concept of financial performance than myopically focusing on just those activities that gave rise to cash this period.

Similarly, firms invest cash in resources like inventory or equipment that will generate benefits for many periods in the future. Accounting spreads out the cost of acquiring the resource over the period it will generate benefits. A lot of what accounting does is "rearrange" cash flows; some cash flows from the past and some expected cash flows from the future will show up in this period's profits.

As with the balance sheet, it is important to understand that income statements are far from perfect in achieving this task. Considerable amounts of subjectivity and judgment are involved in the calculation of income, partly because we can't perfectly predict the future. Not all future period events are allowed to be counted in this period's income (especially if they are very uncertain), and the components of income can vary greatly in how sustainable they are. There are many ways that accounting income can be increased in the short-term at the expense of the long term.

Although the net income number is the "bottom line," focusing solely on this number is dangerous because it doesn't tell you how the income was achieved. A lot of information can be gleaned by looking at the lines above it on the income statement: the types of revenue, the structure of the expenses, the existence of nonrecurring items, and so on. Analysts and others spend enormous amounts of time analyzing income statements to sort these things out to help them make better forecasts of future profitability and better estimates of the value of the firm. This is so important that we'll spend all of chapter 3 on analyzing income statements.

Cash Flow Statement

The cash flow statement is analogous to your bank statement in that it provides information about your inflows of cash (deposits) and outflows (the checks that you wrote that were cashed). It is generally the most objective of the statements. It is able to achieve this objectivity because it looks only at transactions and events that impacted cash this period; it ignores everything else. Either a transaction or event impacted cash or it did not; there is little room for debate.[6] We emphasized the importance of profits in the discussion in the prior section, but cash flow (or liquidity) is also extremely important. That is, running out of cash is obviously not a good idea!

One of the most useful functions the cash flow statement performs is to group the inflows and outflows into three categories:

- Operating activities: collections from customers; payments to suppliers, employees, and other providers of services including interest and taxes.
- Investing activities: payments to acquire long-term productive and financial assets; receipts from disposition of those assets.
- Financing activities: receipts from issuing debt or equity securities; payments to retire debt and payments to shareholders to acquire shares or to pay dividends.

Why is it important to know the sources and uses of cash? If you're generating cash via operating activities versus by selling off your plant, the implications for future profitability are enormous! To be viable in the long run, firms must continue to invest for the future. The investing section of the cash flow statement lets you know how much investing the firm is doing, or whether the firm is contracting by selling off long-term assets. The cash flow statement also provides information about the type of investment; the amount spent to acquire other firms is shown separately from investments in property, plant, and equipment. Keep in mind, though, that only cash investments are shown on the cash flow statement. If you acquire another firm by issuing shares of your own stock or if you acquire the use of assets via a long-term lease, these do not show up on the cash flow statement. For high-tech firms, their most important type of investment is likely to be research and development, but accounting rules do not put these in the investing section (they're classified as operating cash flows instead). Similarly, in some industries, advertising might be considered an investment, but accounting rules require it to be shown in the operating section.

The cash flow statement also tells you where the money is coming from to fund the firm's investments. For young firms and for firms engaged in high-growth strategies, operations are often insufficient to provide enough cash to be able to fund their investments. In fact, for most start-up firms, it's common for cash from operations to be negative. These firms must fund their investments using external financing sources. The financing section of the cash flow statement will tell you what kind—short-term debt, long-term debt, or new equity shares.

More established firms will generally have positive cash from operations and can use some of this to fund their investments. We can see this in Krispy Kreme's cash flow statements. (Although they first became a public firm in 2000, they had been in operation for many decades.)

Table 1.3
Summary statistics from Krispy Kreme's cash flow statement after going public
(numbers in thousands)

	2000	2001	2002	2003	2004	...	2010
Cash From Operations	$32,112	$36,210	$51,905	$82,665	$84,921	...	$20,508
Cash From Investing	$(67,288)	$(52,263)	$(91,640)	$(169,949)	$(47,607)	...	$(8,572)
Cash From Financing	$39,019	$30,931	$50,034	$76,110	$(34,214)	...	$(10,181)

A positive number means an inflow of cash, and a negative number is an outflow. Actual cash flow statements contain much more detail, but we can see from the summary statistics in Table 1.3 that in each year, Krispy Kreme is generating positive cash from operation. However, this is not nearly enough to fund the big investments they are making in order to try to grow. To fill this cash flow gap, they have to use external financing to fund their growth strategy. Note that in 2002 and especially 2003 the amount they were investing grew enormously. In 2004, when their business began to fall apart, new investment was scaled back considerably, and they didn't obtain new financing. Instead, Krispy Kreme's cash from financing was negative; they paid back some of the financing they had obtained in the past. We see a similar set of activities in 2010: operations are generating enough cash to be able to fund new investment and the remainder to pay back financing sources from the past.

This latter scenario is also a characteristic of established successful firms; they generate enough cash from operations to not only fund (most of) their investments, but they also have enough to begin to pay back the financing they had obtained earlier in the firm's life. The financing section will show how much debt is being repaid, how much dividends are being paid, and how many shares are being bought back.

However, even established firms that are generating positive cash from operations will occasionally have a large investment opportunity that requires they seek external financing to help fund. One of the most difficult strategic questions companies must face is how much money to retain on hand, how much to invest in order to build for growth in the future, and how much to pay back to investors and creditors. Having a lot of short-term liquid assets provides safety in the short run. New investment opportunities can suddenly arise, machines can break down, oil prices can rise, and so on. If a company does not keep enough cash (or other liquid resources) on hand, they risk running out of money if something unexpected happens. This can require the firm to resort to expensive emergency financing, selling off assets they would prefer to keep, or in the extreme, default. On the other hand, keeping too much cash on hand means it's not being invested productively, and future profits (and cash) will suffer.[7]

Income versus Cash Flow

Because there is often considerable overlap between cash from operations and net income, it is easy to confuse what they represent. They are not alternative or competing measures of the same thing. In particular, net income is not a measure of cash flow, and cash from operations is not a measure of profitability. The easiest way to see the latter is that when a firm invests in long-term assets, those cash outflows are in the *investing* section of the cash flow statement, not the *operating* section. Yet when the benefits eventually come in from those using those assets, they are classified in the operating section. The operating section never incorporates the costs of long-term assets, only the benefits. The same problem exists with popular performance measures like EBITDA (Earnings Before Interest, Taxes, Depreciation, and Amortization). The benefits from investing in long-term assets are included in this measure, but their cost is not. Moreover, EBITDA does not include interest expense or taxes, both of which are obviously real costs as well. EBITDA can be a useful measure of how well you used your assets, but it is not a measure of the profitability of investing in them.[8] Similarly, cash from operations is a prime indicator of liquidity, which is an important dimension of performance, but it is a different dimension than profitability.

Having said that, another useful role for the cash flow statement is that it helps provide a check on the believability of the firm's profit numbers. If profits are received in the form of cash, you know you have this amount in hand. Profits that aren't cash are more subjective. For example, they may be based on an estimate of how much cash you will collect on credit sales, on how long you will use assets, and on how much you think an asset value has gone up or down. This doesn't make noncash earnings unimportant by any means, but it does suggest that these need to be evaluated more carefully.

How the 3 Financial Statements Relate

The balance sheet equation is one of the most important relations in accounting. In Figure 1.1, we expand the Assets and the Owners' Equity accounts in this equation to separately identify the Cash account and the Retained Earnings account. We do so to help demonstrate the relation between the balance sheet, the income statement, and the cash flow statement. The balance sheet equation has to hold at the beginning of the period (the top of the figure) and the end of the period (the bottom of the figure). How do the two balance sheets relate to each other? One way is through the income statement. In particular, the income statement helps reconcile the beginning and ending balances of the Retained Earnings account:

> Ending Balance of Retained Earnings = Beginning Balance of Retained Earnings + Net Income - Dividends

If a firm is able to generate income and it does not pay it all out as a dividend, the retained earnings balance will go up. But for the balance sheet equation to stay in balance, the net assets (assets minus liabilities) of the firm also have to increase. That is, the amount of earnings the firms has retained has to be invested somewhere in the company. Examining the change in the rest of the balance sheet tells you where.

Similarly, the cash flow statement reconciles the beginning and ending balance of cash, one of the assets accounts:

> Ending Balance of Cash = Beginning Balance of Cash + Cash from Operations + Cash from Investing + Cash from Financing

If the cash balance goes up, for the balance sheet equation to stay in balance there must be corresponding changes in other balance sheet accounts. Investing outflows on the cash flow statement will correspond to increases in the long-term asset accounts on the balance sheet, financing inflows that result from borrowing on the cash flow statement will correspond to increases in the debt accounts on the balance sheet, and so on.

Figure 1.1
Relations between Cash Flow, Net Income, and Changes in Balance Sheets

Balance Sheet at Beginning of Year

Assets = Liabilities + Owners' Equity

Cash + Noncash assets = Liabilities + Contributed Capital + Retained Earnings

Cash Flow Statement
For the Year

Income Statement
For the Year
(minus Dividends)

Cash + Noncash assets = Liabilities + Contributed Capital + Retained Earnings

Balance Sheet Equation at End of Year

Figure 1.1 helps us see what happens if cash flow and income are not the same. Say the firm generates income of $1 million and pays no dividends (so retained earnings goes up by $1 million), but cash flow is only $800,000; that is, the cash account changes by only $800,000. Where is the other $200,000? For the balance sheet to stay in balance, one of the other balance sheet accounts must change accordingly. That is, the difference between cash flow and net income has to be reflected in the change of some other balance sheet account.

Understanding how transactions and events impact the three financial statements and how the three statements are related to each other are such important skills that we will devote the entire next chapter to further developing them.

Chapter 2

Impacting the Scorecard: How and When Actions and Events Affect the Numbers

In this chapter:

- How transactions and events affect the financial statements
- Compiling the financial statements

After four years of falling housing sales due to the persistent recession, Toll Brothers, the largest U.S. luxury homebuilder, acquired land for $143 million in 2010. Despite the fall of housing prices and decline in new sales, Toll Brothers' goal was to anticipate consumer buying trends when the economy bounces back and home sales pick up. What effect did this sizable investment have on the company's balance sheet? Which accounts go up and which go down? How does it impact their cash flow statement? Is it in the operating, investing, or financing section? How (and when) does it affect their profitability? The answers are not as easy as you might think. In fact, the way Toll Brothers will account for this is likely to be different than how your company would account for this same transaction.

Being able to do this kind of analysis is practically second nature to experienced financial analysts and investors. It's also a critical skill for managers to develop. To effectively use financial statements, whether you're an analyst or a manager, you have to understand how they were put together. Accountants take transactions and events and translate them via accounting rules into the financial statements. Managers and analysts then "reverse engineer" this process and use the financial statements to infer what the economic transactions and events were. You can't do the reverse engineering well if you don't understand the principles by which the statements were developed.

A second important reason for understanding how this works is that it will allow you to better project how a proposed strategy will impact the financial statements both for this year and in future years. To do this, you must be able to express how your strategy will unfold in terms of future transactions and events, and to understand how these transactions and events impact the financial statements. Being able to do these things allows you to discuss the impact of your strategy in much more concrete terms and to then be able to use tools of financial analysis to examine all kinds of variations of your proposed strategy to try to improve it.

In this chapter we're going to develop your skills for understanding how transactions and events impact the financial statements. The following are some of the main concepts covered in chapter 2:

- How the balance sheet equation helps structure your thinking for how transactions and events impact the financial statements
- The difference between profits and new investments by owners
- When a cash outflow is an asset and when it is an expense
- How judgment is involved in valuing transactions and events that have future consequences
- How the cash flow statement and income statement are related and how they're different
- How the financial statements are compiled given the underlying transactions and events

How Transactions and Events Affect the Financial Statements

To help cement our understanding of how financial statements are put together, we'll discuss some prototypical transactions and show how they impact the balance sheet, income statement, and cash flow statement. In doing so, we'll see how the three statements are interrelated, as well as how they're different. We'll also use these transactions to highlight a number of the important principles and concepts that underlie accounting rules.

Our discussion will rely heavily on the most important relation in financial statements: Assets = Liabilities + Owners' Equity. Because this relation must always be in balance, every single transaction has to preserve this balance, which means it must also be in balance. This idea is the basis for what is referred to as "double entry accounting": any transaction or event that affects one account must also affect at least one other account; otherwise, the balance sheet equation will no longer be in balance. For example, if an asset account goes up, at least one of the following must also happen: some other asset goes down, a liability goes up, or an owners' equity account goes up. Understanding which one is affected serves as the key to understanding how accounting systems work.

Let's examine the following transactions for a fictional company, Accent Inc., which is beginning its first year of operations. For each transaction, we'll try to assess which asset, liability, and owners' equity accounts are impacted.

A. Shareholders begin a new business, Accent Inc., on the first day of the year. They invest $60,000 of cash in exchange for 2,000 shares of common stock.

Assets	=	Liabilities	+	Owners' Equity
+ $60,000 Cash			+	$60,000 Common Stock

An asset account, titled "Cash," goes up by $60,000. No assets declined, so for the balance sheet to stay in balance the other entry either has to be to increase a liability or an owners' equity account. We don't owe anything to shareholders when we issue them shares, so there is no liability that needs to be recorded. Therefore, the other side of the transaction must be to an owners' equity account, which would typically be named "Common Stock" or "Paid in Capital." This transaction affects cash, so it shows up on the cash flow statement. Specifically, it appears as a financing activity in the cash flow statement.

It is important to note that even though owners' equity has gone up, this is not caused by a profit-oriented activity. That is, we do not recognize this $60,000 as income during the period. A very important role for an accounting system is to distinguish between profit and new investment. To illustrate the importance of this distinction, one major factor that makes Ponzi schemes work (for a while) is that they explicitly violate this rule. They mix together the real profits (which are often low or even negative) with the capital supplied by new investors and claim both are profits. They then pay out dividends from this mix to some early-stage investors (and a lot to themselves) as "proof" of the firm's profitability, then try to repeat this cycle with a new group of investors. To keep the scheme going, they have to continually up the scale of the scheme, until it eventually falls apart.

B. Accent purchases land and a building for $50,000 in cash. Of the total cost, $10,000 is allocated to land and $40,000 to the building.

Assets	=	Liabilities	+	Owners' Equity
- $50,000 Cash				
+ $10,000 Land				
+ $40,000 Building				

Clearly, the asset account, Cash, has gone down by $50,000. In exchange for this cash, we have received two other assets: we increase the Land account $10,000 and the Building account by $40,000. Although both might be grouped together into a Property, Plant, and Equipment account on a balance sheet, the company's records must separate out how much of the $50,000 is attributable to the building and how much to the land. This is done because we will account for the building and land separately after the acquisition date. In particular, the building will get depreciated over time, whereas land (by convention) does not depreciate. Note that although cash has been spent, there is no impact on net income or owners' equity. Accounting distinguishes between cash outflows that are assets (those that still have a future benefit) like this transaction and cash outflows that are expenses (those for which the benefit has been used up or received). This transaction will show up on a cash flow statement in the investing section.

You might have thought that this is how Toll Brothers would account for its purchase of land: increase the long-term asset Property, Plant, and Equipment and decrease Cash, and classify the purchase of land in the investing section of the cash flow statement. This is how most companies would do it. For these other companies, buying and selling land is not their main business. They buy land to put a factory on, they hold the land for decades, and perhaps dispose of it as an ancillary part of their business. For Toll Brothers, this is their main business; they buy and sell land (after putting a house on it) for profit. In financial statements, the classification of items is adapted to fit the type of business the company conducts.

C. Merchandise for resale (inventory) was purchased for $40,000 on account (for credit rather than cash). The goods were marked to sell for $64,000.

Assets	=	Liabilities	+	Owners' Equity
+$40,000 Inventory		+$40,000 Accounts Payable		

An asset account, Inventory, goes up by $40,000. Because we have not paid for the inventory yet, we have a liability to do so. We recognize this by creating a liability account, called Accounts Payable, for $40,000. The transaction does not impact the income statement, and because it does not affect cash, it does not impact the cash flow statement either.

This is, in fact, how Toll Brothers accounts for its purchase of land. For Toll Brothers, their business is to buy land, build a house, and then sell them for a profit. Land is part of their inventory account, and the purchase of land shows up as an operating cash flow on their cash flow statement. The cost of constructing the house is added to the cost of land in the inventory account, and the total is expensed (in the cost of goods sold) when the land is sold. In the next example, we will analyze a sales transaction.

In recording the prior transaction, we ignore the fact that we are intending (hoping) to sell the inventory for $64,000. This is an example of historical cost accounting. The acquisition price is objective and verifiable. The $64,000 intended sales price, on the other hand, is viewed to be too speculative and too aggressive at this point. Revaluing the inventory upward to $64,000 would essentially be tantamount to recognizing the profit on sale now—before we have a buyer, a sales contract, or any cash! Instead, accounting rules force the firm to wait until they actually sell the inventory before profit can be recognized. That profit will be the difference between what they sold the inventory for and what they paid to buy it.

D. Merchandise that had cost $5,000 was sold for $8,000 in cash.

Assets	=	Liabilities	+	Owners' Equity
+ $8,000 Cash				
- $5,000 Inventory				+ $3,000 Retained Earnings

Now we have a sale! The asset account, Cash, goes up by $8,000, and another asset account, Inventory, goes down by $5,000. These two entries alone don't balance, so what are the remaining entries? This difference between what we sold the asset for and what we paid for it is the profit on the sale, $8,000 - 5,000 = $3,000. Retained Earnings is the Owners' Equity account where we accumulate the profits of the firm over time, until such time as they are paid out to the owners as dividends. In fact, another name for the Retained Earnings account is Accumulated Profits. Note even though they are both Owners' Equity accounts, Retained Earnings is being kept in a separate account than Common Stock, consistent with our discussion back in part A. The entries above preserve the balance sheet equation by showing a net increase in assets of $3,000 and a corresponding increase in owners' equity of $3,000. On the cash flow statement, $8,000 of cash was received (and none paid out). Because sales transactions are considered operating activities, we show this $8,000 in the operating section of the Cash Flow Statement.

Technically, firms will actually account for these types of sales transactions in a slightly more complicated fashion. Instead of making the entry directly to Retained Earnings, the firm will set up revenue and expense accounts and keep track of these separately. This will make it easier to construct an income statement, where we want individual line items for the different types of revenues and expenses and not just their total. So what we'd really do is set up a Revenue account within Owners' Equity and increase it by $8,000 (the sales price), and set up a Cost of Goods Sold account within Owners' Equity and decrease it by $5,000; we use a negative number here because this is an expense—it will decrease Retained Earnings.

E. The supplier from whom the merchandise was purchased (in transaction C) was paid $17,000 cash on account.

Assets	=	Liabilities	+	Owners' Equity
- $17,000 Cash		- $17,000 Accounts Payable		

This one is easy. We decrease an asset, Cash, by $17,000, and similarly reduce our Liability for Accounts Payable to the supplier by $17,000. Although cash goes down, this has no effect on income. The income effect is recognized when the inventory we acquired is sold. In theory, this could have already happened, or it might happen in the future, as in the next transaction.

F. Inventory that had cost $15,000 was sold for $25,000. This time, only $6,000 of the sale price was received in cash; the balance is still due as of the end of the year.

Assets		=	Liabilities	+	Owners' Equity	
+ $6,000	Cash					
+$19,000	Accounts Receivable					
- $15,000	Inventory				+$10,000	Retained Earnings

This one is a little trickier than transaction D. Clearly Inventory goes down by $15,000 and Cash goes up by $6,000. The rest of the sales price, $19,000, is in the form of a promise by customers to pay us in the future. This is represented by an asset, Accounts Receivable. Our net assets went up by $10,000, which is the difference between what we sold the assets for relative to what it cost us to acquire them. This difference is profit, and it is recognized by a corresponding increase in Retained Earnings. As before, we would technically initially record this as Revenue of $25,000 and Cost of Goods Sold of $15,000, and then at the end of the year transfer these account balances to Retained Earnings. Note that profit is $10,000, but the cash flow is only $6,000. Part of this difference occurs because we're not paying for the inventory right now, and part of this is because we're not receiving the entire sales price now.

Here the revenue that should be recognized is more debatable. The cash part, $6,000, is in the bank, but there is probably some chance that we won't collect all of the credit sales of $19,000. Accounting rules don't require you to wait until you collect to recognize the revenue; this is viewed to be too conservative and not very timely. Instead, we must estimate the amount of defaults we expect to encounter, and knock down the revenue and the accounts receivable to maintain balance. We'll ignore this in this example.

G. Accent's employees worked and earned total compensation for the year of $4,000. Of this total, $3,000 was paid in cash, and $1,000 will be paid in the future.

Assets	=	Liabilities	+	Owners' Equity
- $3,000 Cash		+ $1,000 Compensation Payable		-$4,000 Retained Earnings

Clearly the asset account, Cash, went down by $3,000 and the Liability account, Compensation Payable, which could be a deferred bonus, vacation pay, pension, and so on, goes up by

$1,000. To balance this, owners' equity has to go down by $4,000. This amount represents an expense for compensation. As in previous examples, it would initially be recognized as an expense account and then transferred to the Retained Earnings account, along with all the other revenue and expense accounts at the end of the year. Note that the compensation expense is recognized on the income statement independently of how much was actually paid in cash. We want to match the total cost to the period when it was earned (which is presumably when we're also getting the benefits from that work), not to when it is paid.

H. Cash in the amount of $2,000 was received from customers on account.

Assets	=	Liabilities	+	Owners' Equity
+$2,000 Cash				
- $2,000 Accounts Receivable				

Easy. Increase Cash by $2,000 and decrease the asset Accounts Receivable by $2,000. There is no effect on income because we recognized the revenue back when the sale was made. We can't recognize it again when we collect, or we would be double counting, which is prohibited.

I. Halfway through the year, the firm borrowed $5,000 from a bank and will pay it back in one year, along with 10% interest.

Assets	=	Liabilities	+	Owners' Equity
+$5,000 Cash		+ $5,000 Notes Payable		

Cash goes up by $5,000, and a liability representing the obligation to repay it, called Notes Payable, goes up by $5,000.

Nothing goes into net income (yet), and the cash inflow shows up in the financing section.

J. A cash dividend of $1,000 was paid to the shareholders.

Assets	=	Liabilities	+	Owners' Equity
- $1,000 Cash				- $1,000 Retained Earnings

The decrease in cash of $1,000 is straightforward. It should also be clear that to keep things in balance, we need a decrease in owners' equity. Paying a dividend to shareholders means that part of the income earned by the firm is no longer retained; it is being paid back to the owners. This is reflected by a decrease in the Retained Earnings account within the owners' equity section. The "tricky" part of this transaction involves understanding that even though it makes Retained Earnings go down, it has no impact on Net Income. Dividends are not an expense; they are not a cost of generating revenues or profits. Instead they are a return of some of the profits back to shareholders. Therefore, to keep track of the balance of Retained Earnings, we need to keep track of the income *and* the dividends paid out. As we'll see, it was probably not a good business decision to pay a dividend at this point in the company's life; the transaction is included just so we can see how the accounting works.

End of the Period Adjusting Entries

These are all the transactions that occurred during the year, but Accent must also assess whether other economic events occurred that must be accounted for. Because there are generally no specific transactions associated with these events, firms must take great care to be sure to include them in the financial statements. The lack of a transaction also means there is often much more subjectivity in evaluating the dollar magnitude of these events.

K. One such event is that Accent used the building (from transaction B) for the year. At the time it was acquired, Accent expected to be able to use it for 10 years before replacing it. During the year, the market value of the real estate in the area increased 8%.

Assets	=	Liabilities	+	Owners' Equity
-$4,000 Building				-$4,000 Retained Earnings

Accent must charge a portion of the cost of the building ($40,000) to this year's income statement. This charge is called depreciation expense. Ideally, the depreciation expense charged off over the asset's life would result in the asset's value at the end of its useful life being equal to its expected disposal value at that time. Let's assume the disposal value is expected to equal zero after 10 years. In that case, a commonly used depreciation schedule, called straight line depreciation, would charge off $40,000/10 = $4,000 of depreciation expense per year. The asset's book value is reduced by $4,000, and the Retained Earnings account is also reduced by $4,000.

Note that we ignore the increase in the local value of real estate. Therefore, the depreciated value of the building does not match the decline (or in this case, appreciation) of the building that has occurred. The "good news" is that this error will eventually get corrected. To see this, suppose we continued to depreciate the building by $4,000 over 10 years so that the book value of the building was zero at that time, but the real market value of the building was $100,000 at that time. If we sold the building then, we'd record a profit on the sale of $100,000 because we sold an asset with a book value of zero for $100,000. Our cumulative profit related to the building over the entire 10-year period we've recognized is then $40,000 of total depreciation expense and a $100,000 gain, for a total of $60,000. This is exactly the difference between what we sold the building for and what we paid for it! Suppose instead we'd only recorded $30,000 of depreciation over the building's life because we expected it to be worth $10,000 at the end of 10 years, but it was worth $100,000 when we sold it. Now we'd record a gain on sale of $90,000 (which is $100,000 minus the book value of $10,000). The cumulative profit over the 10 years is now $30,000 of depreciation and a $90,000 gain, which nets again to $60,000. No matter what depreciation method we use, the cumulative accounting profit will equal the difference between what we sold the asset for and what we paid for it. This equivalence of total cash flow and total accounting profit over the long term is an important property in accounting. The "bad news" is that it can take a very long time for errors like these to correct themselves.

L. Another event that Accent should notice is its use of the $5,000 Note Payable for half a year; the use of that money has some cost (even if we haven't had to pay it yet).

Assets	=	Liabilities	+	Owners' Equity
		+ $250 Interest Payable		- $250 Retained Earnings

At a 10% interest rate, we'll have to pay interest of $500 when the loan becomes due as compensation to the lender for the use of his money. Therefore, a half year's use would cost $250. Stated in another way, if we wanted to pay back the loan now and offered the lender only the original $5,000 we'd borrowed, he would not agree. We'd have to also pay the interest that had been earned over time—the $250. We record this by charging an Interest Expense account that would be a part of Retained Earnings, and we balance this entry by recording a Liability account called Interest Payable for $250. Alternatively, it would also be acceptable to record this liability by simply adding this to the Notes Payable account.

Keep Taxes in Mind

Finally, there is one other expense we need to account for. If we add things up at this point, we'd see that we will have made a profit. Unfortunately, shareholders are not the only ones with a claim to that profit; Uncle Sam is going to want a piece of this too. Therefore, in order to properly measure how much the shareholders' claim has gone up, we need to calculate how much of this will be paid in taxes when they're due in April. Suppose the tax rate is 40%:

Assets	=	Liabilities	+	Owners' Equity
		+ $1,900 Income Taxes Payable		- $1,900 Retained Earnings

As we'll see in the following, pretax income is $4,750. If our tax rate is 40%, we'll owe taxes in the amount of $1,900. To record this, Retained Earnings goes down by $1,900 through an expense account called Income Tax Expense. We haven't actually paid it yet, so cash doesn't go down (yet). Instead, we create a liability account, Income Taxes Payable, to reflect this obligation to pay.

In reality, firms are allowed to keep an entirely different set of books, using different rules for calculating income, for tax purposes than they use for their financial reports to shareholders.

Compiling the Financial Statements

Now we are ready to add up the account balances and put together our balance sheet.

Accents Inc.
Balance Sheet—December 31, 2010
(numbers in thousands)

Assets		**Liabilities and Owners' Equity**	
Cash	$10,000	Accounts Payable	$23,000
Accounts Receivable	17,000	Wages Payable	1,000
Inventory	20,000	Notes Payable	5,250
Total Current Assets	$47,000	Income Tax Payable	1,900
		Total Liabilities	$31,150
Land	$10,000		
Building	36,000	Common Stock	$60,000
Total Long Term Assets	$46,000	Retained Earnings	1,850
		Total Owners' Equity	$61,850
Total Assets	$93,000	**Total Liabilities and Owners' Equity**	$93,000

The balance sheet gives the financial status of Accent at a particular date (December 31, 2010). Looking at successive balance sheets can give you information about how the financial status has changed. Because this is Accent's first balance sheet (its beginning of the year balance sheet was all zeros), in this case the balance sheet is also the change in the balance sheet. Accent's balance sheet tells us that even though Accent started with $60,000 in cash after its stock offering, its cash balance is down to only $10,000. It invested the remainder in acquiring resources, including a building, land, and inventory. In total they have acquired $83,000 worth of noncash assets. They have also racked up some liabilities—a total of $31,150, all of which are due within the next year.

Although we can see that Retained Earnings has increased by $1,850, the balance sheet does not provide a lot of information about how Accent performed during the year. This is what the income statement and cash flow statement concentrate on. Accent's income statement can be constructed by looking at the individual revenue and expense accounts Accent set up.

Accent Inc.
Income Statement for the Year 2010
(numbers in thousands)

Sale Revenue	$33,000
Cost of Goods Sold	($20,000)
Gross Margin	$13,000
Compensation Expense	($4,000)
Depreciation Expense	($4,000)
Operating Income	$5,000
Income Expense	($250)
Pre-Tax Income	$4,750
Income Tax Expense	($1,900)
Net Income	$2,850

Note that Net Income is $2,850, but Retained Earnings only went up by $1,850. The discrepancy occurred because not all of the income was retained by the firm; $1,000 was paid out as a dividend. The line items provided in the income statement are useful because they let us see both the amount of revenue that Accent generated and the structure of the expenses that eat up some of that revenue. In the next chapter we will discuss how to analyze the income statement.

The cash flow statement should be the simplest and clearest of the financial statements, but unfortunately, the way companies present this information makes it much more obscure. In principle, a company would go back through each of the transactions that occurred during the period and check to see which ones involved cash. If a given transaction involved cash, it goes on the cash flow statement, and if not, it doesn't. They would then separate the cash transactions into operating, investing, and financing activities. Finally, within each category they would separate out inflows and outflows. Such a cash flow statement, called the Direct Method, would look like this for Accent:

Accent Inc.
Statement of Cash Flows for the Year 2010
(numbers in thousands)

Cash from Operations	
Cash from Customers	$16,000
Cash Paid to Employees	(3,000)
Cash Paid to Suppliers	(17,000)
Cash Paid for Interest	0
Cash Paid for Taxes	0
Cash from Operations	$(4,000)
Cash from Investing	
Purchase of PPE	$(50,000)
Sale of PPE	0
Cash from Investing	$(50,000)
Cash from Financing	
Issuance of Debt	5,000
Repayment of Debt	0
Issuance of Stock	60,000
Repurchase of Stock	0
Payment of Dividends	(1,000)
Cash from Financing	$64,000
Total Change in Cash	$10,000
Beginning Balance of Cash	0
Ending Balance of Cash	$10,000

This way of presenting a cash flow statement involves a straightforward interpretation. Accent's cash balance went from zero to $10,000 during the year. Both operations and investing activities consumed cash; the cash to fund these came from financing activities, mostly from issuing stock.

The fact that in this example cash from operations is negative yet Net Income is positive demonstrates that liquidity and profitability are not the same thing. The income statement says we generated an increase in value for our shareholders, yet the cash flow statement says this was not received in the form of cash. So where is it? The answer must be that it is on the balance sheet. That is, the balance sheet represents other resources and obligations that have yet to turn into cash.

In fact, most cash flow statements are much more complicated looking than what we have described, particularly in the operating section. Rather than listing the operating inflows and outflows directly, cash flow statements start with Net Income, then make a series of adjustments to "back into" the cash from operations. This is referred to as the "Indirect Method": it produces the same "bottom-line" number for cash from operations but looks different. For our purposes, it is enough to understand what factors impact cash and what section of the cash flow statement they show up in. However, for the interested reader, we explain how the Indirect Method works in the appendix.

Cash flow statements, balance sheets, and income statements operate like scorecards of how well the company is doing. The manager's job is to interpret this data and use it to revise his or her operational, investing, and financing decisions. The past two chapters have discussed what each of the financial statements represents, how they are put together, and how they are interrelated. In the remainder of the book, I describe in more depth how to interpret and use the information. We begin in chapter 3 by focusing on the income statement, which conveys the revenues, expenses, and profitability of the firm (and its subunits).

Chapter 3

Using the Income Statement: Revenues, Expenses, and Profits

In this chapter:

- Getting detailed disaggregate data
- Benchmarks
- Assessing performance, starting with revenues
- Expenses and profitability

Now that we understand how the financial statements are put together, we are in a position to talk about how to use this information for decision making. I'll introduce the most commonly used measures of performance and discuss how to analyze and interpret them. We are going to start by focusing on revenues, then systematically broaden our focus. We'll discuss how to analyze the costs used to generate the revenues; together these determine the firm's profitability. In the next chapter, we'll consider the assets of the firm so we can see whether the firm is using them efficiently. By comparing profits to the assets used to generate those profits, we tie together income statements and balance sheets. Finally, we'll add in the other side of the balance sheet, which tells us about the capital structure of the firm, or the way the assets were financed, and show how this affects performance and risk.

Managers use financial statements for two primary reasons: (1) to help identify where attention should be directed and where corrective actions should be taken, and (2) to help reassess projections about future performance. To do this well, information must be detailed enough to be able to reveal how the "parts" of the firm are doing; summary statistics like net income for the firm as a whole are not sufficient to tell us where we are doing well and where we are not. In areas where we have done well, we want to understand why we've done well. Is this success something we can translate to other areas of the company? Do we want to expand these activities—increase production, build a new plant, open a market overseas? In areas where we've done poorly, why and where did we do poorly? Is it something we can correct? If not, do we want to scale back these activities, outsource them, or stop doing them entirely?

Consider the PepsiCo restructuring example from the introduction. At the time, PepsiCo was composed of three segments: Beverages, Snack Foods, and Restaurants. To make decisions involving these segments individually, they needed to know how each was performing; it is not enough to know how PepsiCo as a whole has performed. As Table 3.1 indicates, PepsiCo measures performance for each individual segment, and their data allow them to compare performance within each segment over time, as well as across segments.

Table 3.1
Selected performance statistics for PepsiCo's segments in 1996

	Beverages	Snack Foods	Restaurants
Sales Revenue (thousands)	$10,524	$9,680	$11,441
Growth in Sales	1.4%	13.3%	1.0%
Operating Income (thousands)	$890	$1,608	$511

All three segments had similar revenue numbers, with the restaurant segment generating slightly more revenue than the other two. However, revenues did not exhibit much growth in either the beverage or restaurant segments. Although each segment earned a positive profit, the restaurant segment had the lowest profits of the three. Therefore, the snack food segment had the lowest revenue but the greatest growth and the greatest profits. The restaurant segment was the opposite; it had the highest revenue but the lowest growth and the lowest profits. PepsiCo ultimately ended up selling off their smaller restaurant chains and spinning off the rest of the restaurant segment into an independent company.

In this chapter on analyzing income statements, we'll cover:

- What benchmarks to use to compare your performance
- Why focusing on revenues is the best place to start financial analysis
- Why growth rate is a heavily emphasized yardstick but not the only important factor
- How to think skeptically regarding your sales
- What gross margins are and why they are a key measure of profitability
- How accounting rules can distort the expenses that show up on the income statement
- Why distinguishing between recurring revenue and expenses versus temporary items is vital in using financial statements to project future performance

Getting Detailed Disaggregate Data

To provide effective support for decision making, organizations must provide managers with data that is compatible with their level in the organization and their areas of responsibility.

Performance measures such as revenue or profit or cash flow can be calculated for each individual segment as PepsiCo has done, and these segments can be defined geographically or by type of product. The numbers can be further disaggregated to calculate performance by product line, by division, by plant, by department, and so on. The lower the level, the more details we want on the performance in each area.

Firms should also be able to supply detail regarding the components of profits: separating out types of revenues and expenses. Production managers will get more details on production volumes, defect rates, and manufacturing costs, whereas marketing managers will find it more valuable to get detailed breakdowns of sales and marketing costs.

Keep in mind that it is beneficial for managers with a primary responsibility in one area to also have an idea of what is happening in other areas. For example, it is very common to break down sales revenue by customer, but far less common to calculate how much profit you are making on a customer-by-customer basis. It is often the case that a small percentage of your customers actually contribute a high percentage of your overall profits. High-revenue customers might not be your most profitable, and in fact can even be costing you money if they are high maintenance. Marketing managers, who are more familiar with the revenues than these extra costs (and who also are likely to be compensated mainly on the basis of revenues) will argue that these customers are valuable to keep, but that is not always the case.

Benchmarks

To assess how good your performance has been or whether something unusual has happened, you need a benchmark for comparison. Perhaps the most common comparison is to your own performance in prior periods. This enables you to see how things have changed over time and helps identify trends or unusual outcomes. For example, much of what appears in the Management Discussion and Analysis (MD&A) section of annual reports compares selected items in the current year's financial statements to the corresponding item from the previous year and discusses why the numbers are different. Comparing your performance to the prior period is also how growth is calculated. As we will discuss, growth is one of the most important and highly scrutinized measures of performance both within firms and in how industry analysts review and value companies.

A second natural benchmark is comparison to other divisions within your own firm or to other firms. Comparing performance to other parts of your own firm helps you to decide where to allocate capital. Comparing to other firms allows you to identify your financial and operating strengths and weaknesses, and helps you to rethink how and where you choose to compete against them; they are probably doing the same.[9] Such a comparison also helps you sort out how much of the change in your performance is due to industry factors (such as an industry-wide slowdown in sales or an increase in raw material prices) or other common factors (such as interest rates) versus a firm-specific effect.

A third common benchmark is the budget. This comparison helps identify surprises, to decide whether forecasts need to be updated, and so on. Regardless of which benchmark is employed, it is useful to discover if the deviation from the benchmark is due to an event that is temporary (nonrecurring) or permanent (persistent). This is an important distinction because a large nonrecurring event is important for evaluating past performance and understanding what happened, but it is less important for looking forward and forecasting future costs and profits.

Assessing Performance, Starting with Revenues

Revenue (or sales) is one of the most publicized and closely examined numbers in the financial statements. Firms often start their quarterly press releases by reporting the firms' sales for the period, and only later do they mention earnings. Revenue is important because it is the end result of all the firm's activities. The financing obtained, the resources acquired, and the goods and services produced are all designed to generate revenue (hopefully enough to cover all of the associated costs). Revenue is more than "the top line" on an income statement; it is also an important determinant of what costs appear on the income statement; many costs are "matched" to the revenue.

Revenues (and expenses) can also be decomposed into their underlying drivers: namely, revenue is sales price times sales volume, and expenses are input cost times the amount of goods or services used. For transactions denominated in foreign currencies, changes in the exchange rate will also impact how these transactions get translated into dollars. Is revenue higher because we sold more products, because the price was higher, or because the exchange rate has changed? If revenue growth is due to the last, we probably should not count on this same growth recurring next year.

Growth in sales is viewed to be a particularly important measure.[10] Why do people pay so much attention to growth? One reason is that growth is often a leading indicator of profits. High-growth firms, therefore, tend to have higher stock prices and Price-to-Earnings (PE) ratios. First-mover advantage in new markets and market share more generally are also related to achieving high growth. Market share, which is usually measured by dividing your sales by total industry sales, is tantamount to providing a measure of how your sales (and sales growth) compares to that of competitors. This is interpreted as a measure of your relative competitiveness as well as of your power and influence in the industry relative to your peers.

But growth can arise from several factors and requires analysis to determine what is generating it. For example, how much of your sales revenues are being generated from new products versus older products? Are certain revenue streams protected via patents so you can count on them in the future? How quickly are those expiring? Are a large percentage of your revenues due to a relatively small number of customers, and if so, what are the financial conditions of those customers and the prospects regarding their demand in the future?

Another useful way to analyze growth is to distinguish between "organic" growth and growth by acquisitions. For example, in the retail industry, it is common to track same-store sales versus sales from opening new stores versus acquiring other chains. The advantage of generating more from existing facilities is that your infrastructure is in place and your costs should not have to increase at the same rate as your revenues do. However, there are limits on how much sales can be expanded in a given store (for example, customers are not going to travel hundreds of miles to shop there) or how much can be produced in a given plant. One of the problems Krispy Kreme encountered by opening so many stores is that their stores began having to compete with each other, not just with other companies. Same-store sales (and profits) began to decline even though sales as a whole increased.

In the case of Vulcan Materials, a producer of construction aggregates, transportation costs are incredibly high. In these cases, acquisitions are an easier way to expand. However, acquisitions are often expensive, as substantial premiums often have to be paid to acquire other companies. To illustrate, in late

2007 Vulcan more than doubled their assets when they acquired competitor Florida Rock, to whom they paid a 45% premium over the existing share price at the time. Vulcan was counting on a rebound of the construction and real estate business in Florida; they're still waiting.

Shrinking sales is often a sign of a shaky financial future, but there are also costs to growing too fast. In some cases, spending to generate the growth gets out of control. Krispy Kreme is a good example, but theirs is by no means an isolated case. As a further example, in his letter to shareholders in PepsiCo's 1996 Annual Report, CEO Roger Enrico offered the following summary of their recent performance, "So what did we conclude? Well, odd as it might sound, we think we simply tried too hard . . . in our quest for growth. Over 30 years, our mistakes have been relatively few, thank goodness, but they've almost always been caused by investing too much money too fast, trying to achieve heroic overnight success where, in retrospect, the odds were tougher than they seemed."

Rapid growth also often means that new people have to be hired and trained, and this can lead to a drop-off in quality and service. Often, management loses the ability to monitor activities as the scale of the firm expands, and this can also adversely affect quality. For example, in 2010, Toyota's president, Akio Toyoda, told a U.S. Congressional committee, "We pursued growth over the speed at which we were able to develop our people and our organisation. I regret that this has resulted in the safety issues described in the recalls we face today."[11] Empirically, firms with the highest growth rates in a short period of time also have a higher probability of going bankrupt than firms with more moderate growth. Companies that grow too fast sometimes end up as shooting stars that skyrocket and then just as quickly fade.

Accounting and Measurement Issues with Revenues

Because managers know that revenue is viewed as an important measure of success, some will take steps to overstate their true revenue. These steps can range from outright fraud to skewing judgment issues to simply being overly optimistic. The pressure to "make the numbers" can sometimes be intense within companies. Keep in mind that the consequences of getting caught can be severe; this is not a road you want to go down.

What are the rules for recognizing revenue? The first important rule is that signing a customer to a contract is not enough to have that contract count in this period's revenue. Instead, the risks and responsibilities of owning the product must have transferred to the customer; he must have economic control of it. These rules exist to try to distinguish legitimate sales from fake ones. As an example of the latter, "bill and hold" arrangements, in which companies take credit for sales even though the customer does not actually want delivery until a later period, is a common way to illegally overstate or accelerate sales. "Side agreements" in which the seller agrees to take the goods back in a following period if the customer does not need them are similar. These types of transactions have been at the heart of scandals for decades, ranging from Sunbeam to Enron. Many of these types of "sales" transactions occur in the last few days of the fiscal period. They are designed mainly to meet sales and earnings targets, either to boost individuals' compensation based on sales or to try to avoid a stock price decline that managers fear might result if the firm misses forecasts made by them or outside analysts. At best, all these actions do is shift sales and income that would have been reported next quarter into this quarter, which leaves you in a hole to start next quarter. The consequences of getting caught manipulating revenue range from discipline within the firm to civil and criminal penalties.

Unfortunately, these types of decisions are so common that revenue recognition is the most frequent area for SEC enforcement actions against companies. Look at the sales transactions that are occurring at the very end of the fiscal period with greater skepticism.

Analyze Credit Sales to Determine Real Revenue

With respect to revenue-related judgment issues, one of the most important relates to credit sales. It is unrealistic to expect all credit sales to be collected, so firms are required to reduce their revenue so that it represents the amount expected to be collected as opposed to the amount that is owed. If a firm sells $100 on credit but they expect 3% of these customers to ultimately default, the firm will recognize only $97 of Net Sales. Similar issues apply to estimating product returns. To find out what your company is predicting for default rates and returns, and especially to find out what competitor firms are doing, you often have to look at the footnotes of the company's financial statements.

Although prior collection experiences within the firm and in similar firms are useful in making this estimation, this is supposed to represent a forward-looking judgment, one based on managers' knowledge of current and expected future economic conditions, as well as managers' knowledge of the credit-worthiness of their customers. For example, in 2008, with the recession, the collapse of the ability of many companies to gain access to credit, and so on, we would expect that companies would raise their assessment of the probability of customer defaults. However, because no one knows the future for sure, some managers purposely overestimate their ability to collect, thereby overstating this period's income. Ultimately, the actual collection experience will be worse than what was anticipated, and the firm will have to write off overstated receivables in the future, thereby lowering future income. Other managers will do the opposite: they'll understate their ability to collect, thereby making what is already a terrible year look a little worse. In this case, when the actual collection experience turns out to be better than what the firm projected, they get to correct their "mistake" by increasing their income in the future. Either way, managers have an ability to shift income across periods through these means.

Delivering the Product or Service: How Bundling Can Affect Revenues

Even if you have received payment by the customer, accounting rules prevent you from recognizing revenue until you have fulfilled your performance obligations to the customer; that is, until you have delivered the product or service. In many cases, it is clear when this obligation has been completed (such as when the customer leaves the checkout line in the grocery store), in other situations, firms bundle multiple products and services into one sales price, but they deliver these goods and services at different dates. Computer software is a common example of this, where software, customization, training, service, hardware, and discounts on upgrades and other products are often bundled together. In these cases, accounting rules require you to divide up the sales revenue across the different "deliverables" and recognize those portions of the overall revenue only when the specific obligations have been completed. Considerable judgment can be required to decide how to appropriately allocate the sales price to the individual services, and how the total revenue gets divided up can make a considerable difference to the company's revenue (and profit) numbers.

To illustrate this point, consider the experience of Apple and its iPhone. When Apple sells its iPhone, it actually bundles two things: the phone itself and the right to receive free software upgrades in the future. The phone is delivered on the sales date, but the free software upgrades is an obligation Apple must supply throughout the standard two-year contract period for phone service. Accounting rules at the time the iPhone was first introduced specified that Apple had to allocate the sales price to the phone and the upgrades on the basis of their relative *actual* sales prices. This was problematic for Apple because they did not sell the upgrades separately. As a result, accounting rules forbade Apple from recognizing any of the sales prices at the time of the sale, even though they had received the cash; instead, they had to spread the entire amount evenly over the two-year phone contract term. This is an example of accounting conservatism, the view that it is "better" to err on the side of recognizing revenue too late than too early. Being overly conservative, however, means the reported revenues were not accurately measuring Apple's underlying economic performance.

In 2009, accounting rules were changed (in part due to lobbying efforts by Apple and other companies) that said Apple could begin to allocate the sales revenue based on *estimated* sales prices; that is, the price the company estimated its sales price would be if they actually sold the service. Apple estimated the right to receive upgrades to be worth $25, and therefore "held back" this amount of the sales price from revenue at the sales date, but recognized the rest immediately. As a result, Apple reported 17% higher revenue and 44% higher net income in 2009 than they would have under the old rules. Although the new rules probably better match the underlying economics of the sales transactions, they also make the revenue more susceptible to manipulation. That is, if Apple changes its estimates of the value of software upgrades (that they don't actually sell), they can shift how much of their sales price is recognized immediately as opposed to being deferred. It is the responsibility of managers to take these kinds of judgments seriously so the numbers that are generated are reliable and provide a sound basis for making good decisions.

Expenses and Profitability

Revenue and growth are important, but they are not the whole story. Growth is not the same thing as profitability. If revenues rise, but expenses rise by even more, profitability suffers. In order to develop and reformulate business strategies, managers must also be able to break down costs. Which costs are high and which are under control? Were profits low because of the effect of a one-time event that caused expenses to be temporarily high, or are the causes more systemic? Analyzing costs generates much-needed feedback on how the company is doing. This information is essential to enable managers to decide how to allocate resources where needed and to decide where cuts must be made. Should we outsource some of the materials or services we use? Is it cheaper to manufacture overseas? Should we introduce a new technology to reduce costs? Choose new suppliers? Are our interest costs getting out of hand, and should we consider refinancing or repaying some of our debt? There are a myriad of costing strategies to select, levers to push, and options to consider that can help make the company more competitive. In this section, we discuss techniques for analyzing your expenses.

Why Analyzing Margins Is Critical

As with revenues, calculating the growth in total expenses, including line item by line item, is a useful calculation. Another extremely valuable tool is to calculate margins. We do this by dividing everything on the income statement by the top line—by revenues. As a result, everything is expressed as a percentage of sales.

For example, using the data in Table 3.1, we can divide the operating profits for each of PepsiCo's segments by their sales to calculate their profit margins.[12] For their snack food segment, dividing $1,609 of operating income by $9,680 of sales means that each dollar of sales translates into 16.6¢ of profits; said another way, PepsiCo spends 83.4¢ in expenses to generate a dollar of revenue in that segment. In their beverage segment, the profit margin is 8.4%, which is roughly half that of the snack foods segment. The profit margin in the restaurant business is by far the lowest at only 4.5%.

Transforming the income statement from dollars to margins is especially valuable in comparing firms and segments that are of extremely different size. The bigger firm will tend to have bigger numbers for all the line items, and this size differential will make it harder to see differences in the structure of the expenses. In fact, another name for the income statement that results once we scale everything by sales revenue is a "common-sized" income statement; it abstracts from the size of the company to better reveal the makeup of your costs.

To illustrate this, let's take our income statement for Accent Inc. from the prior chapter (which we have reproduced in the first column of Table 3.2), and then express it in the second column in terms of margins—by dividing all the line items by sales:

Table 3.2
Income statement and common-sized income statement for Accent Inc.

	In Dollars	As a Percent of Revenue
Sale Revenue	$33,000	100.0%
Cost of Goods Sold	(20,000)	60.6%
Gross Margin	$13,000	39.4%
Compensation Expense	(4,000)	12.1%
Depreciation Expense	(4,000)	12.1%
Operating Income	$5,000	15.2%
Interest Expense	(250)	0.8%
Pretax Income	$4,750	14.4%
Income Tax Expense	(1,900)	5.8%
Net Income	$2,850	8.6%

Looking at the column on the right, we learn that for every dollar of sales revenue, we spent 60.6¢ to pay for the cost of goods sold, which left 39.4¢ to cover all of our other costs and provide for profit. This is referred to as the Gross Margin or the Gross Profits. Gross profits are a key indicator in determining strategy, what to continue to produce, whether prices need to be raised, whether costs have gotten too high, and so on.

Accent then spent 24.2¢ on other operating costs (depreciation and compensation), leaving 15.2¢ to cover our remaining costs. This is referred to as the Operating Margin or Operating Profit. Selling, general, and administrative expenses, and research and development costs would also be included within the calculation of operating margins. Operating costs tend to be less easily matched to revenues compared to cost of goods sold. Finally, interest expense ate up 0.8¢ of every dollar of sales, and income taxes consumed 5.8¢, leaving a profit of 8.6¢ for every dollar of sales revenue.

The common-sized income statement tells the *structure* of our costs. It helps us see how our expenses have changed since last year, as well as how our expenses differ from that of competitors. As expected, the cost structure varies considerably by industry. Manufacturing firms and retailing firms tend to have a high percentage of their costs in the Cost of Goods Sold (COGS). For example, for Dow Chemicals, COGS was 85% of their revenue; for Safeway, it was 72%. On the other hand, for service companies, COGS is much smaller, often close to zero. Delta Airlines, Omnicom Corporation (an advertising company), and Oracle have essentially zero COGS. Instead, their largest costs are in the operating expenses category. Firms with large debt loads will tend to have high interest expense; firms who are able to report their profits in low tax rate jurisdictions will have low income tax expense, and so on.

Accounting and Measurement Issues with Expenses

Keep in mind that accounting rules impact the expenses assigned to the income statement. Consider the Cost of Goods Sold. Accounting systems generally do not keep track of the cost of individual items and then expense those specific costs when those items are sold. Instead, accounting systems often adopt arbitrary cost flow assumptions that are easier to administer (and can have some tax advantages).

FIFO (First In First Out) and LIFO (Last In First Out) are two such systems. The choice between these two accounting methods makes a difference when inventory costs vary over time, which happens due to inflation and other causes. Under a FIFO system, the first items purchased or produced are assumed to be the ones sold, and the later units purchased or manufactured are assumed to be still in inventory. LIFO systems make the opposite assumption. Therefore, FIFO assigns more out-of-date costs to the COGS in the income statement and more up-to-date costs to inventory on the balance sheet; LIFO does the opposite. The real economic condition of the firm is exactly the same either way, but the accounting system makes them look different.[13]

How is this relevant to managers? Consider what happens if costs tend to be increasing over time. Then under a FIFO system, the older costs are being put into the calculation of COGS and being matched to the Sales Revenue to calculate Gross Margin. But older costs are lower costs, which means the Gross Margin is overstated. To illustrate this point, suppose you purchased an item for $1 and later sold it for $5. Your Gross Margin is $4. But does this really mean you have $4 to cover your other costs and provide for profits? What if costs rose between the time when you bought the item and when you sold it, so that it would now cost $3 to purchase a new item? Then once you replenish your item of inventory, you really only have $2, not the reported gross margin of $4, to cover your other costs and provide for profits. This problem is more severe the higher the inflation rate in your costs and the slower your inventory turns over. We will discuss inventory turns (turnover) in the next chapter.

A LIFO system would match a new cost ($3) to the Sales Revenue and report the Gross Margin as $2. Therefore, under LIFO the Gross Margins are up-to-date. However, a different problem occurs with LIFO numbers; this happens when inventory levels fall (for example, when production exceeds sales). This often happens when a firm scales back production to lower their inventory levels because they see future sales as softening. In this case, all of this year's production costs are in COGS and the firm also has to pull items (and their costs) out of beginning inventory. Under a LIFO system, the cost that was assigned to the items being pulled out of inventory can be extremely out-of-date, and the Gross Margin that is calculated on these units sold can be extremely overstated. When this happens, firms are required to report this in the footnotes to their annual report. This requirement alerts investors that the firm will be unlikely to be able to achieve this high a gross profit when they resume production next period and start to sell these units. Sophisticated financial analysts know to check this footnote; you should make sure you check this too. This is important if you are looking at the Gross Margins of other firms to benchmark against yours, and also to verify whether any of these "LIFO liquidation profits" are distorting your own company's Gross Profits.

How Depreciation Affects the Income Statement

For firms with lots of Property, Plant, and Equipment, depreciation is an important expense on the income statement. For most firms, depreciation expense is calculated using the straight-line method. Although easy to calculate and understand, it is unlikely that this method accurately measures the true decline in the value of these assets over time. In fact, assets don't necessarily depreciate every year. For example, a building bought for $2 million could rise in value and be worth $2.5 million five years after being acquired. Accounting statements constructed under IFRS allow this to be recognized; however, U.S. GAAP does not allow you to recognize this appreciation unless you actually sell the building. Historical-cost-based straight-line depreciation can severely distort the real performance of the firm and the value of the assets.

Accounting Rules Are Biased against R&D and Other Intangibles

An even more extreme problem arises with intangible assets and activities such as advertising and research and development (R&D). Accounting rules generally preclude recognizing these as assets. Instead, these costs are immediately expensed in the period in which they are incurred. The rationale for the rule is that these "investments" are too speculative; it is too difficult to reliably link the costs and benefits. But clearly, the reason firms spend money on these activities is because they believe they will generate future benefits.

Accounting rules govern only how the firm reports to shareholders; this does not necessarily make them the best way to run your business. Look at the consequences of immediately expensing R&D (or any of the other types of intangibles) on incentives within the organization. If we conduct R&D, our profits go down immediately because the costs are expensed. The research might yield products that do not generate revenue for many years. Will we (as managers) still be around to get credit for those revenues? If not, what is our incentive to conduct the R&D in the first place?[14] To properly motivate the correct incentives, the managers who incur the costs need to have some expectation of also getting credit for the benefits. Basing performance on the profit numbers produced by an accounting system that expenses these kinds of investments will not achieve this.

Nonrecurring Items

Financial analysts spend a lot of time sorting items on the income statement according to how recurring or nonrecurring they are. This is an important task for managers as well, especially if you are using the financial statements as the starting point for estimating future cash flows and profits. Income statements provide some help in this regard; they separate the bottom-line net income number into sections:

- Income from Continuing Operations
- Income from Discontinued Operations
- Extraordinary Items

Even within the Income from Continuing Operations section, there are many items that vary in terms of how recurring they are. There can be gains and losses from selling plant assets (as opposed to selling your core product), lawsuit settlements, asset write-downs, and so on. As accounting rules become more "mark-to-market" oriented, there can be large "paper" gains or losses that arise when asset values fluctuate over time. Because value changes do not tend to be correlated over time, a large gain or loss one period is unlikely to be followed by a similar gain or loss. Within line items such as cost of goods sold, there can be nonrecurring reasons why costs are high or low, for example, a major repair cost, temporarily high input prices due to weather, and so on.

However, nonrecurring is not the same as totally irrelevant. Many firms go out of their way to downplay the importance of nonrecurring items, especially when they are costs (for some reason, firms rarely seem to have nonrecurring revenues), and even more so when the costs do not involve a cash outlay. Asset write-downs (such as inventory, goodwill, or deferred tax assets) are common examples of these.

For example, when Sun Microsystems took a $2 billion write-down in 2003, their CEO deflected attention from it by saying,

"Sun has had 33 straight quarters . . . of positive cash flow from operations. . . . Cash is king."[15] Similarly, when General Motors took a $39 billion write-down in the fall of 2007, their CEO was quoted as saying, "I think you would have to have a Ph.D. in accounting to understand it. . . . It doesn't have any impact at all. I would encourage people not to overreact in a negative way to it."[16] Investors didn't agree in either case; their stock prices fell significantly on these announcements.

Even "noncash charges" such as these are relevant in estimating future cash flows. To see this, remember that an asset (say, inventory) is a resource that is expected to generate future benefits (such as sales revenue). When we write off that asset, we are saying we no longer expect to receive that future benefit. Therefore, we need to revise downward our forecasts of expected future revenues and cash flows. For both Sun and GM, future years were not the best; Sun ultimately was acquired by Oracle in 2010, and GM had to be bailed out by taxpayers.

Even though the write-off itself is not a cash flow, these future benefits are, and they are relevant for valuation. Moreover, even though this particular write-off probably will not occur again, other write-offs will. If a firm writes off $2.1 billion of inventory (as Cisco did in 2001), it would be silly to project $2.1 billion of additional write-offs for every year in the future. However, it would be similarly silly to project no write-offs ever again in the future. Something in between these two numbers, based on our best estimate of the likelihood and magnitude of future write-offs, makes the most sense to use.

Performing an effective analysis of financial statements requires paying attention to details and investigating to discover the underlying drivers of your performance. This entails asking the right questions and reading between the lines. If profits are low, is it due to low revenues, material costs that were higher than expected, or labor costs that were higher than expected? The corrective action would be very different depending on the answer we find. If we learned the reason is because material costs were higher than expected, is it because prices of material were higher or because we used more materials than expected? If we used more materials than expected, is it because the materials were of lower quality or because we wasted a lot? If the materials were lower quality, was this true for all our suppliers or just one? Is the cause something that is likely to recur in the future, so we should revise our forecasts and budgets for next year? In each step, decomposing performance into its underlying drivers helps identify what the next question to ask is and where to look, and helps you decide what to do to improve performance in the next period.

Chapter 4

Utilizing and Financing Your Assets Efficiently: ROA, ROE, and Leverage

In this chapter:

- Operating performance and return on assets
- Capital structure and return on equity

Contrasting Walmart and Tiffany's is easy. Despite the fact that both companies are retailers, their business models are nearly polar opposites. Walmart is a seller of mostly low-priced groceries, clothing, and household goods, whereas Tiffany's sells myriad luxury items including necklaces, wedding rings, and gifts. Not surprisingly, Tiffany's profit margin (as we defined in the last chapter) is much higher than Walmart's. For example, in 2010 Tiffany's was able to earn 13.1¢ of profit on every dollar of sales, whereas Walmart's profit margin was only 4.2¢. How is Walmart able to compete? The answer is that Walmart is able to generate many more dollars of sales with the assets they invest in their business. In fact, despite their vastly different approaches, both companies earned virtually identical returns on their assets in 2010. How much more effectively does Walmart have to utilize its assets to achieve this? Walmart and Tiffany's also finance their assets very differently. How does the amount of debt they use influence any of these measures?

In this chapter we'll learn why it's important to know how much resources are being used to generate your profits and what factors must be improved to increase your return on investment.

In addition, you will learn:

- What Return on Assets (ROA) and Return on Equity (ROE) are and how they are related
- Why ROA is a critical measure of operating performance
- How ROA and ROE relate to the profit margins discussed in the last chapter
- What the Weighted Average Cost of Capital is and how it sets a benchmark for performance for ROA
- How to assess how effectively you're using assets such as accounts receivable and inventory
- How the way your firm has been financed influences your ROE
- Why the amount of debt you take on increases your risks but can also allow you to leverage high returns to make them even better

Operating Performance and Return on Assets

Profits are an important indicator of success, but we also need to consider how much was invested to generate those profits. For example, profits of a million dollars are not so impressive if the firm invested a trillion dollars to earn them. Shareholders expect managers to use their resources efficiently. If the firm is not generating an acceptable rate of return on the resources made available to them, then they need to redeploy them to some other use. If the firm has no better uses, then they should return the resources to shareholders (via dividends or stock repurchases) and let the shareholders invest them elsewhere.

There are many versions of return on investment (ROI) performance measures, but we'll start with one of the most important: return on assets (ROA). As its name implies, ROA is intended to reflect how effectively we used our assets. In the second half of the chapter, we'll analyze the effects of how we financed the assets, then combine the two factors to show how they jointly impact the firm's return on equity (ROE). As its name indicates, ROE measures how well the firm did for its shareholders relative to their investment. Operating performance (how well you used your assets) and financing performance (how effectively you financed your assets) both impact shareholders' return. It's vital to be able to measure each one separately so we can assess how well we're doing on each one.

We measure ROA using the formula:

$$\text{ROA} = \frac{\text{Net Income} + (1-\text{tax rate}) \times \text{Interest Expense}}{\text{Total Assets}}$$

The denominator is Total Assets. Recall from the Balance Sheet Equation that Assets = Liabilities + Owners' Equity, so Total Assets represents the resources contributed to the firm by both investors *and* creditors. Therefore, the denominator of the ratio does not depend on how the assets were financed, just on the total amount acquired. The numerator in the formula tries to do a similar thing: it represents the profits of the firm before it's divvied up between creditors (who get the interest expense) and the shareholders (who get the rest). We can't simply use Net Income in our formula because interest expense has already been subtracted out in its calculation. So all we're doing is adding it back.[17] We call this unlevering the firm. It gives us the amount that the assets generate for the firm as a whole, before considering how it is going to be split up between investors and creditors.

$$\text{Unlevered Income} = \text{Net Income} + (1-\text{tax rate}) \times \text{Interest Expense}$$

You might see this referred to as the Net Operating Profit of the Firm After Taxes (NOPAT) or Earnings Before Interest (EBI). This measure is especially useful in evaluating the performance of managers whose primary responsibility is operational in nature; that is, people who are responsible for using the assets, not financing the assets.

One additional point to be careful about in calculating ROA (or interpreting it if someone else calculated it) is to check the *date* on which the assets are measured. Income is for a *period* of time, whereas assets are at a *point* in time. What point of time should we use to compare to the income number? It's best to use the average balance over the period because this adjusts for any infusion or withdrawal of assets during the period. If our firm generated $1,100 of unlevered income and had an average asset balance of $5,500, then its ROA would be $1,100 / $5,500 = 20%.

A Benchmark for ROA: Weighted Average Cost of Capital

Is 20% good? What's the right benchmark? As discussed in chapter 3, we could compare the firm's ROA to what it achieved in prior periods or to the ROA earned by other firms in the same period. However, for ROA there is another natural benchmark: the rate of return that investors in the marketplace *expect* to earn. That is, what rate of return do investors expect to be able to achieve on investments of comparable risk?[18] Because the nature of their claims on the profits of the firm differs for debt holders versus shareholders, the riskiness of their claims also differs, and therefore so does the premium for risk they will insist on earning.[19] As a result, we'll refer to the firm as having a cost of debt capital, a cost of equity capital, and a weighted average cost of capital (or WACC—pronounced *whack!*), which is a mixture of the two.

In calculating ROA, our measure of investment is the total assets of the firm. Because the assets have been funded in part by debt holders and in part by shareholders, the appropriate benchmark should weight the required rate of return for each group. To illustrate, suppose our assets are funded 50-50 with debt and equity. If we have to pay 8% on our debt and our tax rate is 35%, the after-tax cost of debt is 5.2%. Suppose the cost of capital provided by equity is 12%. (We'll talk more about this later.) Then the WACC is 0.5(0.052) + 0.5(0.12) = 0.086, or 8.6%. The WACC is the appropriate measure of return to compare to our firm's realized ROA. So in this case, an ROA of 20% is great!

Keep in mind that the WACC will change over time as inflation varies, and it will be different for different firms, and especially for different industries, because their risks are different. It's also important to remember that the WACC applies to the firm as a whole; it does not necessarily apply to each segment of the firm. In particular, if segments differ in riskiness, the higher-risk segments should be held to a higher standard for their expected rates of return.

Improving Return on Assets

How can we make our ROA higher? Whatever strategy we use, it will ultimately have to either increase the amount of profits we generate with a given amount of assets or decrease the amount of assets we need to generate a given amount of profits (or do both). This will involve assessing the ROA of segments of the company to determine where there is room for improvement, as well as evaluating the efficiency in the use of specific groups of assets. At the extreme, this can mean disposing of or selling off assets that are not generating sufficiently high returns. For example, when PepsiCo was making its strategic restructuring decisions in the mid-1990s, the ROA for the prior three years for the snack foods segment was high (17.2%) but the ROAs for the beverage and restaurant segments were significantly lower (7.5% and 5.2%, respectively). PepsiCo decided the returns in the beverage segment could be improved (most of the weakness was outside North America), but they decided to dispose of their restaurant segment.

To be more specific about how to increase ROA, we can decompose it into the following two underlying drivers:

$$\text{ROA} = \text{Profit Margin} \times \text{Asset Turnover}$$

The first term, Profit Margin = Unlevered Income / Sales Revenue, is essentially the same as what we talked about in the prior chapter: how many dollars of profit do we earn from a dollar of sales? The second term, Asset Turnover = Sales / Total Assets, is a new factor; it shows how many dollars of sales we generate per dollar of assets. These two factors interact in a multiplicative fashion (as opposed to additive). This means small improvements in both can translate into a larger change in ROA as a whole.

In comparing these measures across companies or segments, part of the differences will be related to the nature of the products they specialize in. For example, luxury goods tend to have higher markups but lower turnover; some will be due to the competitiveness of the industry. For instance, high competition brings markups down; and some of it represents a strategic choice on the part of the company. The remainder is how well the company is doing in executing their strategy in the competitive environment they face.

This framework also allows us to calculate how to make trade-offs between the two factors in the event both cannot be improved. The Walmart and Tiffany's example discussed at the beginning of the chapter is a good illustration of this. In Table 4.1 we show the profit margin, asset turnover ratio, and return on assets for Tiffany's and Walmart in 2010.

Table 4.1
Comparison of ROA and its determinants for Tiffany's and Walmart

	Profit Margin	Asset Turnover	ROA
Tiffany's	13.1%	0.85	11.2%
Walmart	4.2%	2.40	10.1%

As noted in the introduction, Tiffany's is able to generate more than three times as much profit per dollar of sales. Walmart is able to generate a lot more sales per dollar of assets, but this was not quite enough to make up for the lower profit margin. If Walmart could have generated $2.66 per dollar of sales, its ROA would have been exactly the same as Tiffany's.

To improve the Profit Margin, all of the analysis and discussion in the prior chapter applies here as well to improve ROA. In the next sections, we will discuss how to measure and improve the efficiency of specific assets and continue the comparison of Walmart and Tiffany's.

Turnover of Specific Assets

A useful way to drill down deeper with these measures is to calculate turnover ratios (sometimes called efficiency measures) for specific assets. Two of the most common applications are to accounts receivable and inventory.

Accounts Receivable

The Accounts Receivable Turnover Ratio is designed to measure how quickly you're collecting your receivables. It is defined as follows:

$$\text{Accounts Receivable Turnover} = \frac{\text{Sales}}{\text{Average customer receivables}}$$

For example, suppose a company has sales of $1,095 and has an average receivables balance of $90. We'll use the gross receivables in this calculation, not the net receivables that appears on the balance sheet. In this case, the accounts receivable turnover ratio is $1,095 / 90 = 12.167 times per year. The interpretation of this is as follows: we make $90 of sales on credit, collect that, make another $90 of sales on credit, collect that, and so on, and this cycle of sales and collections would have to repeat itself 12.167 times by the end of the year to generate the $1,095 in sales for the year. That is, the receivables turn over 12.167 times per year.

Equivalently, we can divide this number into 365, and this tells us the average number of days it takes to collect the receivables: 365 / 12.167 = 30 days. This is referred to as the Days Receivables or the Days Sales Outstanding (or DSO). Another interpretation is that each additional $12.167 of sales requires an investment of $1.00 in receivables. This is useful in forecasting future working capital needs.

Because the sales number we use in calculating this ratio typically incorporates both cash and credit sales, the receivables turnover ratio is affected by the mix of cash and credit sales. To illustrate this, the Days Receivables in 2010 was approximately four days for Walmart and five days for Safeway because their sales are almost entirely for cash. That is, sales for cash, checks, and debit cards are all (virtually) the same as cash. If a customer pays with a Visa card, that's also like a cash sale to the company (although Visa keeps a small percentage as a fee); Visa is the one who has the receivable and bears the risk of nonpayment. If the company has its own credit card, then they book a receivable and must wait for the customer to pay. Tiffany has a higher percentage of credit sales, and so their Days Receivables is accordingly higher, slightly more than 20 days. If the mix of cash and credit sales changes, so will this performance measure. For example, Macy's managed its own credit card receivables through the mid-2000s, and their Days Receivables was 40 days during that time. They still have a credit card with their name on it, but most of the operations have been outsourced to a third party. As a result, their Days Receivables has dropped to 5 days.

In other industries, most of the sales are to other companies, not to end consumers, and in those cases most sales are on credit. For example, Days Sales were approximately 60 in 2010 for Dow Chemical. In some industries, the receivables are much longer term: Ford Credit's is over 200 days (car loans), and financial institutions that make home mortgages can have Days Receivables over 10 years.

Ideally, we'd calculate the Days Receivables measure on just the credit sales so that it represents how long it takes to collect, then compare this number to the credit terms we offer to our customers. We'd look for significant year-to-year changes in collection times, or collection periods that are much different from those of our competitors. Higher Days Receivables means longer collection periods and an increased chance of customer default. Long collection times can also be an indication that revenue is being overstated because firms don't tend to collect quickly on fictitious sales. It's tempting to say that our objective should be to reduce Days Receivables as much as possible. In this way, we'd get our money quicker and could then reinvest it in the business. However, it's also possible that we charge a high interest rate on receivables and are therefore quite happy to not get paid quickly. Moreover, offering more flexible credit terms may allow us to make more sales. We have to decide if the greater sales are worth the higher risk of nonpayment and the longer times to collect.

Inventory

We can do the same thing with inventory to calculate how quickly inventory is getting out the door. We define the inventory turnover ratio as

$$\text{Inventory Turnover} = \frac{\text{Cost of Goods Sold}}{\text{Average inventory}}$$

Note that we compare inventory to COGS instead of to Sales, so both the numerator and denominator are expressed in terms of costs. In this way, the ratio does not confound the speed of getting inventory out the door with profit margins. As with the accounts receivable turnover ratio, we can express this in terms of the number of times per year or in terms of how many days it takes us to produce and sell the inventory. As expected, Walmart and Tiffany's have extremely different inventory turnover ratios: Walmart turns their inventory over nine times per year, whereas Tiffany's takes more than a year to turn their inventory over.

In examining our inventory turnover ratio, we look for significant decreases in the number of inventory turns relative to the past or relative to what competitors are experiencing. Possible causes include a reduction in the demand for our product, goods that are out-of-date and/or obsolete, or production problems. These problems can eventually lead to lower profit margins on sales or to incurring losses because inventory has to be written down or scrapped.

We can also drill down further into the components of inventory (raw materials, work in process, and finished goods inventory) to determine how long parts sit around before they're used, how long it takes to complete the production process, and how long it takes completed products to be sold.

Finally, we can add together the Days Receivables and the Days Inventory to get what is called the firm's Operating Cycle:

$$\text{Operating cycle} = \text{Days Receivables} + \text{Days Inventory}$$

This measures the average time it takes for inventory to be produced and sold, and then for the sales revenue to be collected. This is how long our money is tied up in the production and collection cycles. Walmart's Operating Cycle is only 44 days; Tiffany's is 463—more than 10 times as long!

Accounting and Measurement Issues with Assets

When we calculate ROA, the asset number in the denominator should ideally represent an accurate indicator of the profit-generating potential of the assets. However, when we use accounting book values to measure our assets, several factors lead to problems with our measures. These problems will skew the ROA numbers that we calculate and give us misleading information about how well we're doing with the assets entrusted to us.[20]

One potential problem arises if the company uses the LIFO inventory method. In this case, the book value of inventory can be very out-of-date (sometimes decades out-of-date). This generally means that the LIFO value of inventory is much too small, which will make the calculated ROA much too large. Firms are required to report in their footnotes to their annual reports the current cost of inventory. This is generally a much better number to use to try to calculate the real ROA of your assets (and also to calculate the Inventory Turnover ratio).

Property, Plant, and Equipment is generally valued on the books at the original acquisition cost, less accumulated depreciation. The real economic value of the assets, especially for land and buildings, is often much higher. As a result, using the accounting book value of the assets makes the ROA appear much lower than it actually is. This is why managers love assets that have already been fully depreciated for accounting purposes, yet are still serviceable. The ROAs generated from these kinds of assets can be huge because the asset base is so small. Managers often hang on to these assets for longer than they should because once they replace them, the asset base goes way up and their ROA goes way down. Such a decline is not evidence of a bad economic decision; it's purely an accounting artifact. More on this follows.

Calculating ROA using book values for the assets is even more problematic for intangible assets because there is a good chance those intangible assets do not even show up in the listed assets. Yet these intangible assets could be the major driver of your revenues. For example, in 2009, Coca-Cola generated an ROA of 15.9%, a very respectable return. However, this number is based on the average value of their assets as reported on their balance sheet, which was $45 billion. As we have discussed, Coca-Cola's balance sheet does not include their brand name, which has been estimated at $70 billion. If we included this number in their asset base, Coca-Cola's ROA drops to 6.2%, a far less impressive number. When we don't try to measure these intangible assets in our performance measures, it's hard to tell if we're doing things to preserve (or increase) the values of our intangibles.

Before we leave this section, it is important to emphasize that performance measures like ROA only reflect performance for one period. One bad year does not imply that an entire strategy should be scrapped. When a firm implements a new strategy that involves heavy investments, it's very common for ROA to drop initially. This is because the investments usually precede the returns, often by many years. Even if we delay recognizing the costs of the investments on the income statement until the benefits come in, the investment costs are on the balance sheet. As a result, they're in the denominator when we calculate ROA. Because there are no returns yet, ROA will go down until those benefits are eventually realized. We have to take a longer-term perspective on performance than myopically focusing on each year (or even worse, each quarter) if we want to make the decisions that are best for the firm.

Capital Structure and ROE

So far we've talked about Return on Assets (ROA) and its determinants. Remember that this is what is available to *all* the suppliers of capital—both investors and creditors. How much of this do shareholders get? The answer depends on the capital structure of the firm; that is, the mix of debt and equity. Debt holders supply some of the capital the firm uses to acquire assets. In return, some of the money that the assets generate goes to debt holders in the form of interest payments. Shareholders get the rest. We call the return the shareholders get on the amount they invested the firm's Return on Equity (ROE), which is defined as:

$$\text{Return on Equity} = \frac{\text{Net Income}}{\text{Stockholders' Equity}}$$

The profitability measure is Net Income; this is the return that goes to the shareholders. Similarly, the investment measure is what has been provided by shareholders. As with ROA, it is preferable to use the average balance for Stockholders' Equity throughout the period in order to take into consideration the inflow or outflow of shareholders' investment throughout the period.

A Benchmark for ROE: Cost of Equity Capital

What's the relevant benchmark for an acceptable ROE? Because there are no explicit payments owed to equity holders, a common misconception is that equity capital is free. This is completely wrong; the relevant rate of return is the amount that shareholders could get in the marketplace for investments with identical risk. Because the claims of debt holders get paid first, equity is a riskier claim than is debt. Therefore equity investors demand a higher rate of return as compensation for this risk; equity capital is more expensive than debt capital. This means the benchmark for ROE is generally higher than the WACC.

There is less agreement as to how to measure risk from the perspective of equity holders than there is for debt holders. One of the most widely used approaches, called the Capital Asset Pricing Model (or CAPM for short), is based on the idea that some risks are diversifiable and some are not. Diversifiable risks are those that can be greatly reduced (or even eliminated) by shareholders by holding a well-diversified portfolio of firms. Therefore, these risks are not priced in the marketplace; shareholders do not demand an extra premium to invest in firms whose profits are affected by these kinds of risks or uncertainties.

For example, consider the risk imposed on a transportation company, such as an airline, by uncertainty in the price of oil. High oil prices hurt them, but low oil prices help them. This may be an important risk to a manager of the transportation company, but it is less important from the perspective of its shareholders. The reason is that shareholders can easily reduce their exposure to this risk by holding a portfolio that consists of both transportation companies and oil producers. Whichever way oil prices move, profits by one group will tend to be offset by losses in the other group. The idea that diversification helps reduce exposure to risk is the driving force behind the investment advice "don't put all your eggs in one basket."

What risks aren't diversifiable? In the extreme, it's the portion of a firm's profits that move with everyone else's profits. That is, it is the extent to which your profits move with the economy as a whole. Firms whose profits go up greatly in bull markets and plummet steeply in bear markets are viewed to be high-risk firms. Investing in these firms can't help much to diversify the risks of an investor's portfolio because they move the same way as all his or her other stocks.[21] On the other hand, firms whose fortunes do not rise and fall as sharply when the market as a whole moves are viewed to be less risky. Gold, soft drinks, and utilities are examples of industries that are less impacted by how the rest of the economy moves.

Comparing ROA and ROE

How do ROA and ROE compare? If the firm has no debt, they're identical. However, if the firm has debt (and interest expense), ROE could be either higher or lower than ROA. As we'll see, the relation depends on (1) how much the firm is able to earn on its assets relative to what it has to pay out in interest, and (2) how much debt the firm uses. We refer to these effects as being attributable to leverage. Similar to the use of this term in physics, leverage is something that will amplify an effect. Leverage will make good times even better, but it will make bad times even worse. We illustrate this in the following example:

Firm A and Firm B have identical assets that earn exactly the same rates. However, their capital structures differ; Firm B is more highly levered.

	Firm A	Firm B
Total Assets	$8,000,000	$8,000,000
Total Debt	$2,000,000	$4,000,000
Total Equity	$6,000,000	$4,000,000
Total Capital	$8,000,000	$8,000,000
Interest Rate on Debt	10%	10%

Now let's look at what happens if we vary the profitability of the underlying assets. We'll consider the impact on firms A and B if we change the (pretax) return on assets from 5% to 10% to 15%. Specifically, we'll look at their Net Income and their ROE. We'll walk through the first case (Firm A's assets earn 5%) in detail; the others are similar. If Firm A earns 5% pretax on $8 million of assets, that's operating income of $400,000. From this they have to pay interest of 10% on $2 million of debt, which adds up to interest expense of $200,000. This leaves $200,000 of pretax income. If the tax rate is 35%, then they have to pay $70,000 in tax, which leaves $130,000 in Net Income for shareholders. Because shareholders' investment was $6 million, their ROE is 2.2%. Note that the interest expense shows up before the income tax line because it is a tax-deductible expense.

If Firm A's assets earn a higher rate of return, then Firm A's operating income goes up, but its interest expense doesn't change. All the extra income goes to shareholders (net of the taxes on this extra income). Accordingly, ROE goes up as well. For Firm B, the calculations are similar, except Firm B has more interest expense because it has more debt. Firm B's Net Income is therefore lower in each case than the corresponding income for A. We could make a case that the interest rate on Firm B's debt should be higher than Firm A's, which would make Firm B's income even lower. However, Firm B's investment by shareholders is also lower. As we see, Firm B's shareholders don't get any return in the worst-case scenario, but they do better than Firm A in the best-case scenario:

Effect on Firm A:	Pretax ROA = 5%	Pretax ROA = 10%	Pretax ROA=15%
Operating Income	$400,000	$800,000	$1,200,000
Interest Expense at 10%	200,000	200,000	200,000
Income Before Taxes	200,000	600,000	1,000,000
Income Tax Expense at 35%	70,000	210,000	350,000
Net Income	$130,000	$390,000	$650,000
ROE = Net Income / Equity	**2.2%**	**6.5%**	**10.8%**

Effect on Firm B:	Pretax ROA = 5%	Pretax ROA = 10%	Pretax ROA=15%
Operating Income	$400,000	$800,000	$1,200,000
Interest Expense at 10%	400,000	400,000	400,000
Income Before Taxes	0	400,000	800,000
Income Tax Expense at 35%	0	140,000	280,000
Net Income	$0	$260,000	$520,000
ROE = Net Income / Equity	**0.0%**	**6.5%**	**13.0%**

Now let's present these same numbers in the form of a graph in Figure 4.1. The less steep line represents the ROA for Firm A (the less highly levered firm), and the steeper line represents the ROA for Firm B (the more highly levered firm).

Figure 4.1
Effect of financial leverage on return on equity

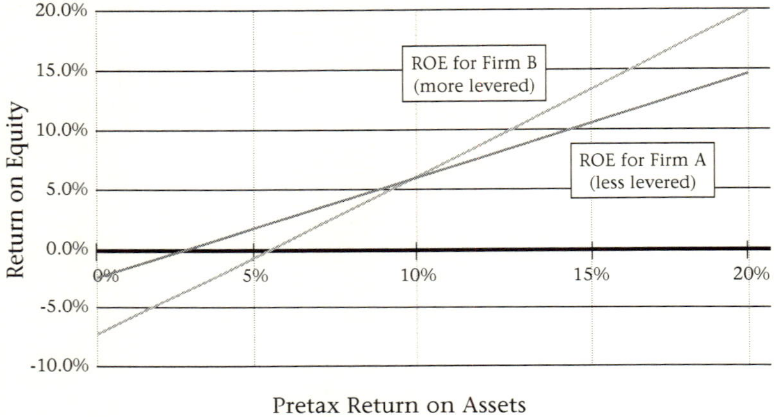

What do we learn from this graph and these calculations? If the firm's return on assets is exactly the same as the interest rate it pays out on its debt (10% pretax, or 6.5% after tax), the amount of debt it has (or the amount of leverage it takes on) does not matter. All of the extra money the firm generates by funding some assets with debt goes back to the debt holders; none of it goes to shareholders.

However, if the firm can earn more with its assets than it is paying out on its debt, the firm's ROE is above its ROA. The shareholders get to keep the extra money without having had to contribute any investment of their own to get it, so their return on their own investment goes up. Moreover, the more debt it has, the more this difference is magnified. Firm B (the more highly levered firm) does better than Firm A in this range.

On the other hand, if the firm happens to earn less with its assets than it is paying out on its debt, the firm's ROE will be less than its ROA. Now the shareholders have to kick in some of their own return to pay off the promised return to debt holders. In this case, the more debt the firm has, the worse off the shareholders are. Firm B does worse than Firm A in this range.

One of the major implications of these results is that higher leverage makes Firm B's equity riskier than Firm A's. We can see this in three ways:

(a) It has a larger hole to start out in. That is, it has $400,000 of interest costs to cover instead of Firm A's $200,000.
(b) It must earn a higher pretax return on its assets to break even (earn zero profits) than Firm A must. We'll discuss break-even points in more detail in chapter 5.
(c) Its ROE is more sensitive to underlying fluctuations in its operating income and return on assets.

As a result, investors and creditors use leverage ratios, like the debt-to-equity ratio or debt-to-asset ratio, as some of their most important predictors of risk and financial distress. Firms with higher leverage ratios, other factors being equal, have to pay higher interest rates to borrow money.

How Much Debt?

How do you decide how much debt you should take on? It's clear that debt has a downside: it increases the chances of bankruptcy. What's the benefit? One benefit is that the interest you pay out on debt is tax deductible. In contrast, returns you pay out to shareholders in the form of dividends or share repurchases are not tax deductible to the firm. Firms that have low tax rates (nonprofits, firms with large losses, and so on) don't get much in the way of tax benefits from debt, so they don't use a lot of debt to do their financing. Firms with relatively safe (low volatility) cash flows can afford to take on more debt because they have a low probability of a really bad outcome that would lead to default. Public utilities back in the days of rate regulation were a good example of this. Finally, firms with assets that are largely tangible often borrow more. The reason is that tangible assets are something the lender can take control of or repossess in the event the borrower defaults. It's harder for a lender to take possession of intangible assets, especially goodwill. The ability to take possession of an asset provides the lender with additional protection and lowers the interest rate they'll charge to earn an adequate return. The lower interest rate makes borrowing money more attractive to the firm.

Leverage is a double-edge sword. It can be a way to earn spectacular returns. If you buy a firm and improve the ROA—the efficiency of the use of assets—your return is amplified if you financed the purchase with a lot of borrowing. This is the principle behind Leveraged Buy-Outs (LBOs). Many hedge funds use lots of debt as part of their strategy. On the other hand, highly levered firms are the ones most vulnerable to an economic downturn. They don't have enough of a buffer of equity to be able to absorb losses if sales slow.

Accounting and Measurement Issues with Debt

Some companies try to fool investors by using accounting loopholes to try to hide their liabilities by keeping them off their balance sheet. This is referred to as off-balance-sheet financing. They do this to make their debt-to-equity ratio look lower, and therefore give the impression that they are less risky than they actually are. They hope this will allow them to borrow money at lower rates than their real risk would warrant.

Historically, leasing has been a popular way for companies to try to keep some of their debt off their balance sheet. The buy-versus-lease decision can be a complex one that involves many factors. Leasing is often a more flexible and inexpensive way to acquire the use of assets, especially for short periods of time. However, continuing to renew short-term leasing arrangements can in the long run be more expensive that it would have been to purchase the asset outright. Taxes and who bears the risk of obsolescence and changes in market value of the underlying assets are also important considerations in designing lease contracts. Rather than making the leasing decision, and the design of the structure of the lease contract, solely on the basis of these kinds of business factors, accounting factors have also played a major role in leasing. Accounting rules allow some types of leases, termed operating leases, to receive favorable treatment. In particular, the obligation to make future payments under the leasing contract does not show up on the firm's balance sheet as debt. Firms therefore go to great lengths to get their leases to qualify as operating leases to keep these obligations off their balance sheets. Accordingly, we have seen enormous increases in the number of operating leases entered into over the years.

Smart investors and creditors are aware of this trick, so they in turn spend considerable time trying to put these obligations back on the books before they start crunching the numbers to assess credit-worthiness. This game of "hide it and try to find it" is not very socially efficient. Fortunately, accounting rules are finally wising up to this game so that more leases will be put "on the books." Once the new rules take effect, the accounting effect of the leasing decision will (hopefully) be less important, and the decisions can be made more on the basis of the real business effects.

The recent bankruptcy examiner's report on Lehman Brothers brought to light another trick financial institutions (and probably many other firms) were using to keep debt off their balance sheets. This trick exploits the fact that balance sheets represent the financial status of the firm *on a specific date.* For example, only the amount of debt we have on December 31 matters on our annual report. Suppose we sell some assets on December 29 and use the proceeds to buy back debt by December 31. Our leverage ratio calculated using the December 31 balances will go down, and we'll look less risky. We can then reverse those transactions on, say, January 3 to restore debt to the more typical level, and that doesn't show up on our balance sheet as long as we unwind it again just before the end of the next period. This is all perfectly legal, although misleading.

Lehman Brothers tried to do this without actually selling their assets and buying them back. Specifically, they used securities as collateral in a complicated borrowing transaction termed a repo (which is short for repurchase agreement). In doing so, they took advantage of an accounting loophole that said that if you posted extra collateral in a repo, you could account for this as if you sold the securities and held a financial derivative contract to buy them back. There is no legitimate business purpose in posting more collateral than you need to secure a loan other than to get this favorable accounting treatment. The legality of this is still being determined by the courts.

To minimize the risk of getting embroiled in these kinds of controversies (and lawsuits), you should always try to ask yourself what business purpose is served by designing a transaction or contract in a particular way. If the primary answer is there isn't one, and you're just doing it that way because of the accounting treatment or because it makes your numbers look better, then you might want to rethink if that is really the right way to do it.

In this chapter, we've developed a framework for understanding the factors that drive financial performance and how these complex factors interact. We showed that the return on investment made by shareholders, termed ROE, is a function of the operating performance of the firm's assets as well as the financing performance of the firm, as measured by its leverage. The operating performance of the assets, measured by the ROA, can be further decomposed into an asset turnover ratio and the profit margin on sales. This links the analysis in this chapter to what we did in the last chapter, where we focused on profit margins. We also described how to measure the efficiency of the use of assets. Finally, we described the costs and benefits to taking on additional debt, in order to determine the optimal capital structure for the firm.

Chapter 5

Using Cost Information in Decision Making: Know How Your Costs Behave

In this chapter:

- Cost-Volume-Profit (CVP) analysis
- Special orders and classes of customers
- Resource constraints
- Allocated costs
- Why sunk costs are irrelevant (or should be)

After teetering on bankruptcy and being bailed out by the federal government, General Motors still recognized in 2011 that it needed to slash cuts or face extinction. Not only would it have to produce energy-efficient, fuel-efficient, quality automobiles, but it had to do so at a cheaper price to stay competitive. GM spent $600 million to overhaul its small car assembly plant in Orion, Michigan. Landfill gas will supply about 40% of the plant's power, generating savings of $1.1 million annually. Greenhouse gases and other environmental hazards are expected to be substantially reduced. GM also negotiated reduced pay of newly hired union workers, who will now earn $14 to $16 an hour, about half the pay rate of older workers.[22] Performing its cost analysis and subsequently reducing its cost of producing automobiles has contributed to GM's ability to bounce back from near extinction.

But GM isn't the only company that has had to rigorously analyze its costs. Indeed, all companies need to dissect their costs and constantly reformulate new strategies to stay competitive.

Accounting rules require firms to classify costs according to their function. This is because only certain types of costs are allowed to be inventoried—namely, those costs necessary to bring the product to a completed state. For a manufacturing company, this would include production costs (materials, labor, and overhead), but not selling, general, and administrative (SG&A) costs. We can clearly see this distinction on income statements because these costs are shown on separate lines. This classification of costs is useful for some purposes, but other ways to categorize costs are even more valuable for decision-making purposes. The ability to "slice and dice" your costs and understand how they behave will allow you to make better decisions. What factors make your costs change? How much will they change?

Some of the major topics about cost analysis covered in this chapter include the following:

- The importance of distinguishing fixed costs from variable ones
- Understanding the role of contribution margin in determining profitability
- How to calculate a break-even point
- The danger of relying on full costs per unit in decision making
- Finding ways to sell and discount "excess capacity" to produce additional revenue
- How cost allocation procedures can distort product profitability
- What sunk costs are and why they're irrelevant

Cost-Volume-Profit (CVP) Analysis

Suppose the following income statement represents our performance last month, and we're predicting that sales volume will drop by 10%. Will our profits also go down by approximately 10% to $3,600? The answer is almost certainly not, even if our underlying cost structure remains the same. In fact, we're likely to do far worse than $3,600.

Revenue	$80,000
Cost of Goods Sold	($55,000)
Gross Margin	$25,000
Selling, General, & Administrative Expenses	($21,000)
Profit	$ 4,000

The estimate that profits will drop 10% implicitly assumes that all our costs move proportionately with volume. Another way of saying this is that all our costs are variable costs. This is rarely descriptive.

Instead, most cost functions are better described as containing a mixture of fixed and variable costs. Fixed costs are ones that do not change as activity levels, such as sales volume, fluctuate. On the manufacturing side (and included in the Cost of Goods Sold line in our example) would be things like factory rent, much of the depreciation on manufacturing plant and equipment, supervisor salaries, and so on. Similarly, within Selling, General, & Administrative (SG&A) there are also fixed costs, such as depreciation on office buildings, salaries for marketing and sales personnel, and so on. In contrast, variable costs do change with activity levels. Variable manufacturing costs include materials, direct labor, and certain kinds of factory overhead, such as power. Variable SG&A costs would include commissions, shipping costs, and so on.

If we can separate out our costs into fixed and variable ones, we can get a much better estimate for how our profits behave.[23] Suppose we determine that our costs are as follows:

	Fixed	Variable
Manufacturing Costs	\$35,000 per month	\$2 per unit
SG&A Costs	\$11,000 per month	\$1 per unit

Then at a sales volume of 10,000 units, our manufacturing costs would have been \$35,000 + (2 × 10,000) = \$55,000, which is the number in the income statement last month. Similarly, SG&A costs would be \$11,000 + (1 × 10,000) = \$21,000, which also matches the income statement line item for SG&A.

Now suppose sales volume drops by 10% to 9,000 units. What will happen to our revenues and costs?

Revenues will be	\$8 × 9,000	=	\$ 72,000
Manufacturing Costs will be	\$35,000 + (2 × 9,000)	=	(\$53,000)
SG&A Costs will be	\$11,000 + (1 × 9,000)	=	(\$20,000)
Profit		=	(\$1,000)

So we'll actually lose money if sales go down by 10%! Our profits go down a lot more quickly than we thought when sales volume drops. Now that we know how our costs behave (we graph revenues and costs as a function of volume in Figure 5.1), how do our profits change with volume? Generalizing the previous calculation:

Profits = (Sales price – VMC per unit – VSC per unit) × Volume – FMC – FSC

Where VMC = Variable Manufacturing Cost

VSC = Variable SG&A Cost

FMC = Fixed Manufacturing Cost

FSC = Fixed SG&A Cost

The expression in parentheses in the previous equation is called the Contribution Margin per unit. This is the amount by which the sales price covers the additional variable costs to produce and sell that unit. That is, this is the amount that each unit contributes to covering all the fixed costs and ultimately to making profits. For our example, the contribution margin (CM) per unit is \$8 – 2 – 1 = \$5 per unit. In our initial speculation about what would happen to profits, the reason we were mistaken is because we implicitly assumed that profits changed at the rate of 40¢ per unit (which is the monthly profit of \$4,000 divided by that month's volume of 10,000 units), when in fact they change by \$5.

Armed with this information, we're now able to calculate how profits vary with any given level of sales volume:

$$\text{Profit} = \text{CM per unit} \times \text{Volume} - \text{Total Fixed Costs}$$

If we graphed Profit as a function of Volume, we'd see that when volume is zero, profit is the negative of the total fixed costs, –\$46,000. This is the intercept of the graph in Figure 5.2. For every unit we sell, profits go up by the CM per unit, or \$5. This is the slope of the line in Figure 5.2.

The equation above can be used to estimate the profit of any given volume. We can also turn the relation around to determine what volume we'd need to achieve a given level of profits. Of particular interest is the volume level that allows us to exactly break even.

Setting profits in our equation above to zero and solving for Volume gives us:

$$\text{Break-Even Volume} = \frac{\text{Total Fixed Costs}}{\text{CM per unit}}$$

That is, the break-even point is the volume where the total contribution margin exactly covers all the fixed costs. In our

Figure 5.1
Revenue and cost as a function of volume

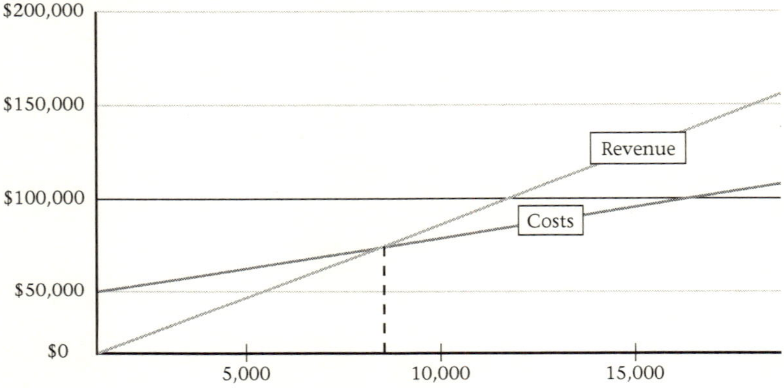

Figure 5.2
Profit as a function of volume

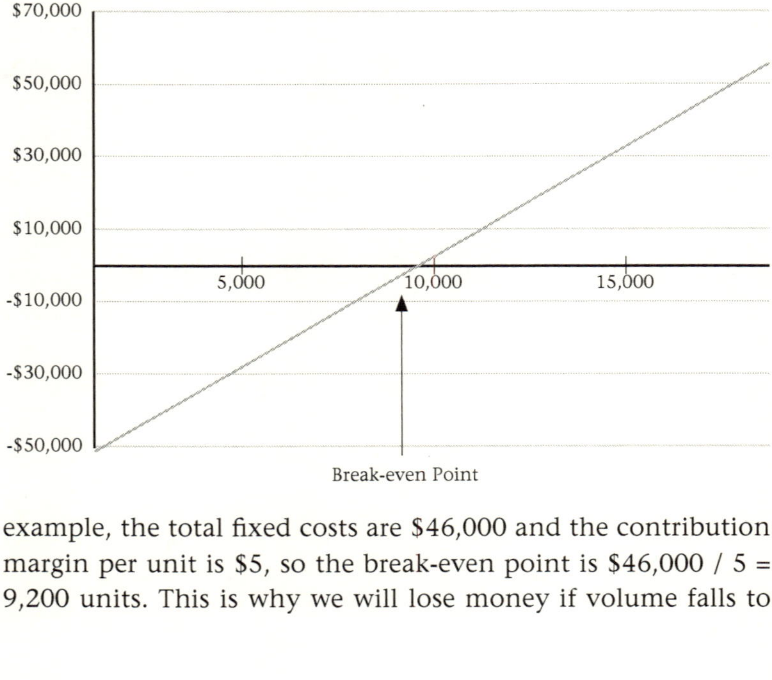

example, the total fixed costs are $46,000 and the contribution margin per unit is $5, so the break-even point is $46,000 / 5 = 9,200 units. This is why we will lose money if volume falls to

9,000: it is below the break-even point. In fact, it's 200 units below the break-even point, so at $5 per unit, that's a loss of $1,000, just as we calculated.

This calculation also allows us to see what our "margin of safety" is; that is how much of a sales drop relative to its current level we could absorb without incurring a loss. In our case, sales can fall only by 800 units relative to the 10,000 level we're at now; the margin of safety is 8%.

Understanding the relation between costs, profits, and volume helps a variety of decisions. It is most important in assessing the profit potential of new ideas, projects, and products. Ask yourself how much you could realistically expect to sell. Then calculate the break-even point to see if you're going to be anywhere remotely close to this. Often, the answer will be no. In this case, you need to scrap the idea or think of some other way to deliver the product with a considerably different cost structure.

Cost-Volume-Profit analysis is well suited for use in spreadsheets, where it is particularly easy to conduct sensitivity analyses. This involves varying the underlying assumptions regarding sales prices, costs, and volumes to see what happens to profits. What happens under best-guess, optimistic, and pessimistic scenarios?

Cost behavior information also allows us to examine alternative ways to produce the product. These production technologies will result in different combinations of fixed costs and variable costs per unit. For example, suppose that by making a large investment in automated equipment, our variable cost of producing an extra unit goes down. Is it worth the incremental fixed costs? The answer is likely to depend on the anticipated volume level. At high volumes, the variable cost per unit is the more important characteristic, whereas at low volumes the fixed cost tends to be more important. The Profit-Volume graph allows us to make these comparisons more precise.

The revenue and cost functions we used previously were linear in volume. The assumption of linearity gives us a relatively easy-to-understand formula. However, there is nothing to prevent us from incorporating more complicated (and realistic) nonlinear functions into the analysis. For example, some costs might go up in "steps" as we have to add capacity to achieve more volume. Revenues could be nonlinear because we eventually have to lower price to achieve greater volume. All of this can be easily built into a spreadsheet model. We won't be able to get things to reduce to a nice equation like we could in our example, but we can still calculate everything numerically and perform all the sensitivity analyses we like.

Special Orders and Classes of Customers

Another useful application of these techniques is in evaluating special orders and alternative pricing for different classes of customers. For example, suppose our sales manager approaches us with an order request from a new customer who is willing to pay $7 per unit. Should we take it? Our immediate reaction might be to turn it down because it is below our normal selling cost of $8. Another reason to turn it down is that it's less than our costs (our costs last month were $7.60 per unit), so we'll lose money on the job. But on closer inspection, that's not the case. In fact, we learned that each additional unit costs only $3 to produce and sell (the variable costs).

The rest of the $7.60 per unit number we had calculated comes from "unitizing" our fixed costs. That is, we divided our fixed costs of $46,000 by last month's volume of 10,000 to arrive at a fixed cost per unit of $4.60. This is a highly misleading number; it makes sense only at a volume of 10,000. If volume is higher, fixed costs don't go up by $4.60; they stay exactly the same. As volume goes up, the fixed cost per unit goes down; the fixed costs get spread over more units. For this reason, it's always dangerous to rely on "unit costs" to make decisions; you're much better off looking at total costs to estimate how costs and profits will change.

From our analysis, we know that any price we receive above the variable cost per unit of $3 will add to our profits. This is therefore the absolute minimum price we would be willing to accept on this special order. Whether we should accept or not also depends on what impact accepting this job will have on other revenues; in particular, how much (if any) will it cut into our regular sales at our normal $8 price?

Many industries have devised ways to sell their "excess capacity" at lower prices. Hotels and airlines are good examples of industries where this is a common problem. The hotel room is sitting there empty, the plane is going to fly with empty seats; the marginal cost of an additional hotel guest or an additional plane passenger is very low. In these industries, companies have figured out (with the help of other companies such as Priceline, Orbitz, and so on) how to get some contribution to profits from these otherwise empty rooms and seats by selling them at highly discounted prices. Restaurants do the same thing by offering reduced prices before 6:00 p.m. Automobile dealers and retailers do similar things with their end-of-the-season sales. In these industries, companies count on the fact that not all customers can wait until the last minute or the end of the season or model year, or don't want to eat dinner at 4:30 p.m., so that offering these deals still allows them to sell enough of their goods and services at the regular price. If a similar issue exists with our regular customers in our example, accepting the special order could be profitable even though it looks at first glance like a money loser.

Resource Constraints

Now let's suppose we have two products, and based on what we learned in the prior sections, we've already dissected the costs and calculated the contribution margin of product A to be $5 per unit and the contribution margin of product B to be $3 per unit. Suppose both products require the use of a common resource, which has only a limited capacity. For example, suppose a production machine has a maximum number of hours it can be used in a month, and both products require its use. Where should we allocate the capacity: to producing product A or B? Because A has the higher contribution, that's the better choice, right?

But what if you could produce twice as many units of product B in the same amount of time as product A? Then the contribution margin per unit of output is not the relevant comparison. Instead, the relevant measure is contribution margin per unit of the constraining resource. It if takes, say, one hour to make a unit of product A, then we can make $5 per hour of machine time if we devote that hour to product A, but because it only takes a half hour to make a unit of product B, we can make $3 / 0.5 = $6 per hour of machine time if we devote it to product B. Therefore, with these contribution margin per hour figures, we can see that we should allocate as much machine time as we can to satisfying the demand for product B. Only if we still have capacity left after satisfying product B's demand should we devote any machine time to product A.

Note that this analysis also tells us the marginal benefit of expanding our machine capacity (say, by buying additional machines). For every additional hour we can supply, the extra benefit is $6 if we're still trying to fill all the demand for product B, but it falls to $5 if we're already able to fill the demand for product B and are now trying to supply customers with product A.

When there are multiple types of resource constraints, the idea is the same but the optimal produce mix is more complicated to solve. There are mathematical programs that will solve for the optimal product mix and also give you an indication of the value of adding capacity at different places to relieve the resource constraints. Such an analysis can help you identify where the most serious bottlenecks are in your operations, so you can focus on reducing or eliminating them in order to improve the efficiency of your processes and increase your profits.

Allocated Costs

Another problem that makes using cost and profit numbers challenging is that they often contain (arbitrary) allocations of costs. To illustrate this, suppose we have a company that is expecting to break even in terms of overall profits. They have two products (or divisions), and they want to see how each is doing. They know to distinguish between fixed and variable costs, so they've calculated the following profitability numbers:

	Product 1	Product 2
Contribution Margin Per Unit	$2 per unit	$5 per unit
Anticipated Sales Volume	30,000	15,000
Total Contribution	$60,000	$75,000
Fixed Costs	$70,000	$65,000
Profits	($10,000)	$10,000

Product 2 is making a profit, but not product 1. By dropping product 1, the managers think they can raise corporate profits because they'll avoid the $10,000 loss product 1 is expected to generate. They'll certainly lose product 1's revenues, but will they avoid the costs? In particular, will the firm's fixed costs really go down by $70,000 if they drop product 1?

There are many reasons why the answer might be no, but a common one is that product 1's cost structure contains the allocation of shared costs or corporate-wide costs that likely will not change if product 1 is dropped.

Suppose the details of each product's fixed costs are as follows:

	Product 1	Product 2
Avoidable Costs	$55,000	$53,000
Allocated Factory Overhead Costs	9,000	4,500
Allocated Corporate Overhead Costs	$6,000	$7,500

For each product, some fixed costs are avoidable; they are specific to that product and they can be eliminated if we shut down that product line. However, other costs represent costs incurred at another level (perhaps the factory or the corporate level) that have been allocated to the two revenue-generating products. In the numbers above, factory overhead has been allocated on the basis of units of production, which is why product 1 gets twice as much. Corporate overhead has been allocated on the basis of sales revenue, so more of it goes to product 2. If product 1 is shut down, the firm will not save the overhead costs being allocated to it. Those corporate and factory functions still exist and the same costs will be incurred. If there is no product 1 to allocate some to, they will simply be reallocated to product 2.

Shutting down product 1 will therefore result in a loss of its $60,000 contribution margin, but will result only in the avoidance of $55,000 of fixed costs. That is, shutting down product 1 will actually cost us $5,000. All the corporate and factory overhead costs being allocated to product 1 now, $15,000, would be reallocated to product 2. This will make product 2 now show a loss of $5,000, so we might be inclined to also shut it down. But if we did that, we'd lose even more money! In a company with more than two product lines, this can be a vicious cycle that continues while you drop more and more product lines at each step, forcing the others to shoulder the burden of the factory and corporate overhead costs.

Allocated costs are often a large part of product costs. The allocations are frequently made on fairly arbitrary bases and do not reflect the amount of resources and costs actually consumed by the product or division. More sophisticated costing systems (such as activity-based costing) exist to try to make these allocations on more of a cause-and-effect basis, but these systems are more expensive to administer. Be careful about trusting the accuracy of allocated costs; examine the structure of your costs so that you understand which ones will actually change as a function of your decisions. In this example, unless corporate and factory overhead costs can also be slashed when you shut down product 1, it's best for the firm to keep it going.

Why Sunk Costs Are Irrelevant (or Should Be)

Suppose you acquired an asset for $1,000 a few years ago that you're trying to decide what to do with. Your two strategies are as follows: you can sell it for $3,000 now or continue to use it to produce products over the next several years. If you adopt the latter strategy, you estimate that the economic value you will generate is $2,400 (netting incremental future costs and considering the time value of money). The asset won't be worth anything after that. Clearly, you would be better off selling the asset now; $3,000 of benefits is greater than $2,400. Equivalently, if we net the original acquisition cost, a cumulative profit of

\$3,000 – 1,000 = \$2,000 is greater than profits of \$2,400 – 1,000 = \$1,400. Either way we look at it, the strategy of selling now makes us \$600 better off than if we keep using it.

Would things be any different if you had originally paid \$10,000 for the asset instead? The answer should be no; all you can do now is make the best decision possible going forward from where you are now. What you paid for the asset, which we refer to as a sunk cost, cannot be changed at this point. The profitability is lower for each strategy, but the strategy of selling now is still exactly \$600 higher than that of keeping the asset. You might wish you hadn't paid so much for the asset in the first place, but you can't undo that decision now.

Unfortunately, this is not how the decision usually gets made. Getting rid of the asset is essentially admitting you made a mistake in acquiring it in the first place. Accounting systems and performance evaluation systems often exacerbate these kinds of issues. Selling the asset now results in a loss showing up on the income statement now; it reveals that, in hindsight, a bad investment decision had been made. However, if you keep the asset, you don't have to write off its costs immediately, and you can delay the recognition of the loss. In order to avoid taking a hit to your reputation (or your annual bonus), you make a decision that is bad for the firm: keep using the asset. Sunk costs are often not treated as irrelevant by the person who sunk them! Interestingly, the opposite behavior tends to happen if a new manager comes on board who did not make the original investment decision. The new manager would be much more inclined to take a loss on the investment and blame it on his predecessor, thereby enabling him to start with a cleaner slate and making it easier to show improvements the next year (which he takes credit for).

The lesson from the last example is that the past cash flows and future cash flows must be distinguished. In the next chapter, we carry this idea further and analyze how to evaluate strategies whose cash flows differ in terms of when in the future they occur.

Chapter 6

Evaluating Investment Opportunities: Discounted Cash Flow Analysis

In this chapter:

- A framework for calculating the economic value created by your strategic decisions
- Applying present-value techniques to an investment decision
- Higher-level strategic decisions

In June 2011 Google, which is primarily known as an Internet company, invested $280 million to finance the production and installation of solar home panels. Although solar provides only a tiny percentage of the power needs in the United States and is often considered too expensive for most homeowners to invest in, Google believes that some time in the future its $280 million investment will pay off. Indeed Rick Needham, Google's director of green business, explained, "We make investments that make business sense and we are comfortable with the return given the risks."[24]

Almost all important business decisions involve evaluating activities that result in cash flows that occur at different points in time. Indeed, the definition of an investment is an activity that requires a cash outlay now to generate inflows in the future. Despite the risks associated with plowing capital into new projects, companies must invest to grow and prosper. Older projects eventually peter out, so in order for a company to keep growing and remain profitable, it must constantly reinvent itself. Companies are like farmers that must plant the seeds for next year's crops. Of course, a company has many different types of investments to choose from, including buying new equipment, building plants, acquiring competitors, developing new product ideas, and investing in intangible assets, such as hiring more people. Moreover, it can invest in new lines of business or start marketing to different audiences, including overseas. The possibilities are nearly endless. These strategies vary considerably in the amount of investment they require, the speed with which they generate returns, and their riskiness. In this chapter, we'll discuss the important tools for evaluating these kinds of decisions. In addition to investment projects, this framework is also used to value long-term liabilities, such as bonds and pensions. Wall Street analysts use these same techniques to value firms. This framework is also useful in many personal finance situations, such as taking on and paying off a mortgage, saving for your retirement, for your children's college tuition, and so on. We'll cover the following points:

- Why present value (discounted cash flow analysis) is the proper framework for calculating the desirability of decisions that involve cash flows at different points in time
- How to calculate present values
- How big a return an investment has to generate in order to be worthwhile
- How the length of time the project takes to generate its benefit impacts its profitability
- How to incorporate risk into the analysis
- Common pitfalls in estimating future cash flows

A Framework for Calculating the Economic Value Created by Your Strategic Decisions

How do you compare the returns from all the possible kinds of investments? The key idea in this chapter is understanding the time value of money; dollars at different points in time are different economic commodities and therefore cannot be treated interchangeably. This is the exact same idea as dealing with different currencies. If you bought something for ¥76,000, spent $300 to transport it, and sold it for €2,000, it's obvious that you can't simply add up these numbers to determine what your profit or loss was. Instead, you have to convert them all to equivalent terms, and you'd use market exchange rates to do that.

The same idea applies to dollars that are paid and/or received at different points in time. You can't simply subtract the amount you invested 5 years ago from the return on that investment today to calculate the investment's profitability. In the same way that markets exist to exchange different currencies, markets also exist to exchange dollars at different points in time. These exchange rates are called interest rates. We can see that dollars at different points in time are not the same by observing that these exchange rates are not one-to-one; that is, interest rates are generally not 0%. This means a dollar today is not worth the same economically as a dollar a year from now (or 10 years from now, and so on). If you ignore this fact, you'll make plenty of bad economic decisions.

Moving money back and forth over time is an everyday occurrence. To move money from the future to now is called borrowing. To move money from the present to the future is called investing (or lending). Present-value techniques are what allow us to meaningfully compare dollars at different points in time, and interest rates are the rate of exchange. For example, if you could invest a dollar today and earn an interest rate of 8% per year, you'd have \$1.08 at the end of the year. Therefore, if you knew you could move money back and forth over time at a market rate of interest of 8%, you'd be indifferent between the right to receive a dollar now and the right to receive \$1.08 a year from now. If you don't like the one you get, you can always exchange it for the other: they are of equal value.

Similarly, if you could invest \$1 at 8% per year for n years, you'd have accumulated a total of $(1.08)^n$. Note that future values don't go up linearly with time; they go up at a faster and faster rate. This is the effect of compounding interest: in the later periods, you earn interest not just on your original dollar but also on the interest you'd earned to date. More generally, if you can invest \$1 today at r% interest per year, the amount you'd have n years in the future would be $(1+r)^n$. This is referred to as the future value of \$1 at r% in n years.

We'll usually find it more useful to do the reverse of this procedure, which is called taking the present value. That is, if we were offered \$1 to be received a year from now and the interest rate were 8%, the current value equivalent of that future dollar is \$0.926, or 1/1.08. To see this, note that if you borrowed 92.6¢ today and invested that at 8%, you'd be able to pay back 0.926 × 1.08 = \$1.00 at the end of the year. Therefore, the present value of \$1 a year from now at 8% is 92.6¢. Similarly, \$1.00 to be received two years from now is equivalent to \$0.8573 today. More generally, the present value of \$1 to be received n years from now at an interest rate of r% per year is $1 / (1+r)^n$, or equivalently $(1+r)^{-n}$. The farther out in the future we go, the less a dollar received then will be worth. This is why we refer to future dollars as having to be discounted; they're worth less than a dollar today.

To apply this concept to projects or other types of decision-making scenarios, we have to be able to express the project in terms of the stream of cash flows that the project will generate or affect. As we'll see, the present value of the project's stream of cash flows measures the economic value added or reduced by that project. A project that generates a series of cash flows that has a positive present value is one that adds value to the firm; if the present value of the cash flows expected to be generated by a project is negative, that project reduces firm value. In comparing two different projects or sets of activities, the one that generates the highest present value is the one that adds the most economic value and is the preferred project for the firm. Done correctly, these calculations incorporate the magnitude of the cash flows, their timing, and their risk so that we are able to properly compare projects that differ along these dimensions.

To operationalize present-value techniques, we'll break the process into three steps. We'll briefly describe each step now, then go into each in more depth in the rest of the chapter. As we'll see, these techniques are particularly well suited to be done on spreadsheets.

1. Lay out a timeline of the cash inflows and outflows that relate to the project.

This step requires you to specify not just the magnitude but also the timing of future cash flows. As an example, consider a decision we are contemplating that will result in the following stream of cash flows, where C_t is the cash flow in period t.

Time Period:	0	1	2	3	...	T
Cash Flow at time t	C_0	C_1	C_2	C_3	...	C_T

We'll denote an inflow of cash to us as a positive number and an outflow as a negative number. By convention, period 0 is the present, period 1 is one period from now, and so on.[25]

This timeline must include *all* of the cash flows that are affected by the decision we're evaluating. Cash flows for the firm that are unaffected by the decisions we're evaluating can be left out of the analysis. In some cases, the timing and magnitude of the cash flows are specified by a contract (such as with a bond). In most other situations, these cash flows have to be estimated. This is generally the most challenging part of the analysis and the one you'll spend the most time on.

2. Choose an interest rate (often called a discount rate) to apply to these cash flows.

The appropriate discount rate to use is the rate that you can earn in other investments of equivalent risk. When dealing with external markets, this is the market rate of return. Within firms, the rate is often referred to as a hurdle rate or the cost of capital. Although firms are free to use whatever rates they want internally to help them decide which projects to choose, ideally these should be chosen to be consistent with the rates of return demanded in the outside market. In principle, the appropriate rate of return depends on (among other things) the riskiness of the project. Higher-risk projects require a higher rate of return to justify their adoption. Therefore, not all prospective projects in a firm should have their cash flows discounted at the same rate. The discount rate will generally be given to you by the accounting and finance departments; as a nonfinancial manager, it's unlikely you'll be expected to determine the appropriate discount rate. For simplicity, in our discussion we will assume the discount rate is constant over time; however, the techniques are perfectly capable of handling time-varying discount rates.

3. **Convert the cash flows in each period to their equivalent value in some common time period (usually the present) and add up the converted values.**

This is called taking the present value. Once you get comfortable with these problems, this step will generally be the easiest part. Calculators and spreadsheets have numerous present-value functions built into them. All you need to do is point to the cells in your spreadsheet where the future cash flows are, tell it what discount rate you want to use, and it does the calculation automatically.

Applying Present-Value Techniques to an Investment Decision

We can apply present-value techniques to cash flow streams that vary over time in any pattern, but we'll consider the prototypical investment scenario in which a cash outlay is made now with the expectation of future benefits. We'll start with a simple example and then increase its complexity (and realism). The simpler setting will also make it easier to see why it is economically sensible to look at present values.

Consider the Google example at the beginning of the chapter, and suppose we are thinking of buying one of the solar panels. Assume solar panels of the size we're interested in cost $10,000, which we'll pay for now in cash. The benefits will come in the future from reduced electric bills. The value of these benefits will depend on how sunny it is, the price of electricity, and how long the panels last. We'll vary the nature of these benefits as we work through the problem to illustrate the key ideas. To start as simple as possible, let's initially suppose that we expect to get benefits for only one year, and that we've estimated we'll save $10,500 on our electric bill during the first year (the bill is paid at the end of the year). No other cash flows in the firm are affected.

Based on this information, if we invest in solar panels, the cash flows of our firm will change as follows:

Time Period	0	1
Cash Flow at time *t*	-$10,000	+$10,500

We have to make a cash outlay of $10,000 now (period 0), and in return we'll get a cash savings of $10,500 a year from now (period 1). This seems like a good deal; we make a $500 profit, right?

But our analysis hasn't taken into consideration the time value of money yet. Suppose we could invest our money elsewhere (or suppose shareholders can) and earn 8% in investments of equal risk. Now the $10,500 savings on our electric bill doesn't look so attractive. If instead we took our original $10,000 investment and invested it elsewhere at 8%, we'd have $10,800 at the end of the year. With that, we could pay the electric bill of $10,500 and still have $300 dollars left over to spend on other things (or pay out as a dividend). Therefore, investing in solar panels is a poor investment decision in this case.[26]

Being $300 richer a year from now (by investing elsewhere) is not the same as being $300 richer today. As before, we can use present-value techniques to convert to an equivalent value today. With interest rates at 8%, we saw that $300 a year from now is the same as $300 / 1.08 = $277.78 today. Therefore, the decision to invest in solar panels makes us $277.78 dollars worse off today.

We can do this same calculation more simply by just taking the present value of the original cash flow stream, as follows:

Time Period	0	1
Cash Flow at time *t*	–$10,000	+$10,500
Present Value of Cash flow at time *t*	–$10,000	$10,500 / 1.08 = $9,722.22

Total Present Value: –$10,000 + $10,500 / 1.08 = –$10,000 + $9,722.22 = –$277.78

The cash flow right now (at period 0) of $10,000 is already in present-value terms, so we don't need to make any adjustments to it. The cash flow of $10,500 received at the end of period 1 has to be discounted back one period to convert it to equivalent dollars today, so we divide that cash flow by 1.08. This tells us that the cash savings of $10,500 in the future is really only worth $9,722.22 today. This is less than the initial cash outlay by $277.78, so this is the net economic loss we'd incur by investing in this project.

How big would our electric bill savings have to be to justify this investment? The answer should be obvious: it has to be at least $10,800, the same as what we can earn by investing elsewhere. An equivalent way to say this is that the investment in solar panels has to earn at least an 8% return, which is our cost of capital. In our original example, a $10,500 return on our investment of $10,000 is only a 5% return. Because this project's return is less than our cost of capital, this makes it a money-losing project.

Now let's change the nature of the benefits. Suppose everything is the same as in the previous example, except we're expecting $5,500 of benefits a year for two years. Note that the total benefits of $11,000 not only exceed the initial cost of the panel, $10,000, but it also exceeds the threshold level of benefits, $10,800, that would have made this an attractive investment in the initial example. This doesn't necessarily make this a good deal now, however, because the benefits are more stretched out over time. When the cash flows are spread out over longer periods of time, they have to be larger to make the investment worthwhile. A longer period of benefits also makes it harder to tell simply by looking at them whether or not the present value is positive. To find out, let's do the calculation:

Time Period	0	1	2
Cash Flow at time *t*	–$10,000	+$5,500	+$5,500
Present Value of Cash flow at time *t*	–$10,000	$5,500 / 1.08 = $5,092.59	$5,500 / 1.08^2 = $4,715.36

Total Present Value = –$10,000 + $5,092.59 + $4,715.36 = –$10,000 + $9,807.95 = –$192.05

As before, the initial cash outlay is already in present-value terms, so we don't have to adjust it. The first year of savings on our electric bill has to be discounted back one year, so we divide that cash flow by 1.08, and we see that the $5,500 of cash savings a year from now is equivalent to $5,092.59 today. The second year of cash savings has to be discounted back two years, so we divide by 1.08^2, and this shows that the $5,500 of cash savings in the second year is equivalent to only $4,715.36 today. This is far less than the first year's savings were worth. The further out in the future we go, the more that cash flow will be discounted. Overall, our calculations show that we'll get benefits that have a present value of $9,807.95, which is less than the original investment cost. In this case, the project lowers our economic value by $192.05.

To verify the intuition behind present-value techniques, let's calculate what would happen if we invested our $10,000 elsewhere and earned 8%. At the end of year one, we'd have $10,800. We could pay our electric bill that year of $5,500 and have $5,300 left. We could then take the $5,300 and invest it one more year at 8% and have $5,724 at the end of year 2. This is more than enough to cover that year's electric bill; it leaves us $224 at the end of year 2. Moreover, $224 two years from now is the same as $192.05 today, which confirms our original calculation. Whether you express things in terms of their future value or their present value, investing in solar panels isn't a good decision here.

This is the beauty of present-value calculations (and markets). Suppose we have two projects, A and B, and the present value of project A's cash flows is higher than the present value of project B's cash flows. A higher present value means we can use markets to borrow and lend to transform project A's cash flows in a way that exactly duplicates project B's cash flows and leaves money left over (in whatever period we like). This means project A is the preferred project. Even if we don't like the timing of cash flows that A generates, we can always use capital markets to alter the timing to one we like better of equivalent value. The project with the highest present value is the preferred project.[27]

Now what if the benefits last 3 periods, or 10, or 20? As you can imagine, these kinds of calculations can get tedious. Rather than doing the present value of each cash flow individually, this is where calculators and spreadsheets come in. For the special case where the cash flows are level over time, which is called an annuity, mathematicians have worked out that the present value of the annuity can be characterized as a formula:

$$\text{Present Value of Annuity} = \$A\frac{[1-(1+r)^{-n}]}{r}$$

where r is the discount rate, n is the number of periods the annuity lasts, and A is the amount of the cash flow per period.[28] This formula is also built into financial calculators and spreadsheets. In Excel, for example, the formula for the present value of an annuity is called PV, and its inputs are the discount rate, the number of periods, and the annuity amount.[29]

To illustrate, suppose the benefits of investing in solar panels will last 5 years, and we expect to save $2,800 per year.

The present value of the cash flows can be calculated one by one as above:

Time Period	0	1	2	3	4	5
Cash Flow	-$10,000.00	$2,800.00	$2,800.00	$2,800.00	$2,800.00	$2,800.00
Present Value of Cash Flow	-$10,000.00	$2,592.59	$2,400.55	$2,222.73	$2,058.08	$1,905.63

and we can add these up to get the total present value:

Total Present Value = –$10,000 + $11,179.59 = +$1,179.60

Or we can note that this stream of payments is one cash outflow of $10,000 followed by an annuity of $2,800 a year for 5 years. Using the annuity formula (via the formula above or a calculator or a spreadsheet), we can calculate that an annuity of $1 a year for 5 years discounted back at 8% is 3.993, so the total present value of the cash flows is the same number as above:

Total Present Value = –$10,000 + PV of annuity of $2,800 a year for 5 years @ 8%
= –$10,000 + $2,800 × 3.993
= –$10,000 + $11,179.59 = +$1,179.59

Note that in this case, the present value of the cash flows is positive, which means that this project adds value to the firm. Equivalently, we could *not* take our investment of $10,000, invest it elsewhere at 8%, and duplicate this stream of cash savings that investing in the solar panels will generate. This must mean that our project earns a higher rate of return than 8%. What rate does it earn? To calculate this, we have to determine the rate of return that would allow us to take our initial investment and exactly duplicate the stream of cash flows this project offers. More generally, it is the discount rate that would cause the project's entire stream of cash flows to have a present value equal zero. We refer to this as the project's Internal Rate of Return (IRR). We can calculate this via trial and error, or use calculator or spreadsheet functions to do it. In Excel, the function is called IRR, and to use it you have to supply it with the spreadsheet cells that contain the entire stream of cash flows. The IRR in our example is 12.4%. The statement that a project earns a rate of return higher than the cost of capital (8%) is equivalent to saying that the project has a positive present value (discounted at the cost of capital of 8%).

Now let's add some commonly encountered complexities into the analysis. First, we'll incorporate inflation, then taxes. Then we'll consider issues that arise in higher-level strategic decisions, where many more line items are involved.

Inflation

A common mistake is to make your estimates of future inflows and outflows based on prices and costs as they exist *today*, and simply apply them to the future sales and input quantities. In our last example, we assumed that the savings in electricity was a constant $2,800 a year for five years. This savings was implicitly based on multiplying two factors: our estimate of the savings in kilowatt hours we'd otherwise have to buy elsewhere in each year and the price of electricity that year. Even if the kilowatt hours saved was constant over time, is it reasonable to expect prices to stay the same? In most industries, prices and costs evolve over time. The most common reason is inflation, which causes prices and costs to trend upward over time. If we don't incorporate inflation into our estimates, we will usually significantly understate the present value of the project's cash flows.[30]

For example, suppose that after the first year, we expect electricity prices to go up by 5% per year. This means our savings in year 2 will be \$2,800 × 1.05 = \$2,940, our savings in year 3 will be \$2,800 × $(1.05)^2$ = \$3,087, and so on. As we can see in the following table, this makes the present value of our benefits much higher than we originally projected.

Time Period	0	1	2	3	4	5
Savings @ Year 1 Prices		\$2,800.00	\$2,800.00	\$2,800.00	\$2,800.00	\$2,800.00
Inflation Adjustment Factor		1	1.05	1.1025	1.157625	1.21550625
Projected Savings		\$2,800.00	\$2,940.00	\$3,087.00	\$3,241.35	\$3,403.42

Inflation increases the value of the benefits as we move forward in time, which partially offsets the discounting of those cash flows. The present value of these benefits, when discounted back at 8%, is now \$12,262.53, which makes the overall present value (netting the initial cost) \$2,262.53. The project's rate of return increases to 15.9%. Note that the cash flows are no longer constant over time, so we cannot use the formula for annuities. Fortunately, calculators and spreadsheet programs like Excel also have functions for these more complicated patterns of cash flows.[31]

Obviously, higher inflation rates or a longer period of time that inflation persists will make this effect bigger. In decisions that involve multiple types of revenues and expenses, remember that not all of them will go up at the same rate. In fact, in many high-tech industries, prices and costs often come down over time instead of going up.

Taxes

Don't forget taxes! If our profits are higher because our electric bill is smaller, we'll have to pay more taxes. Taxes can be a significant cost, often eating 30% to 40% of your profits. Incorporating taxes is more complicated than simply multiplying the pretax cash flows times the tax rate. Taxes are based on the income numbers you report to taxing authorities, not based on your pretax cash flows. This timing difference is important because the time value of money is the major focus of our discussion in this chapter.

Often the area where this makes the most difference relates to investments in property, plant, and equipment (PPE). The amount you spend to acquire PPE is generally not deductible on your tax return in the year in which you spend it. Instead, you depreciate this investment cost systematically over time on your tax return. Therefore, you don't get the tax benefit from this cash outlay until later. The same total amount eventually gets deducted, but the deduction is spread out over time instead of being received all at once.

To illustrate this, suppose the tax rate is 30%, and consider our $10,000 investment in solar panels. If that amount were immediately deductible, our taxes would be lower by $3,000 immediately. Instead, this asset gets depreciated over its useful life. This means we won't get the $3,000 deduction right away. The tax code specifies the useful life and depreciation method you're supposed to use for different classes of assets. Typically, these depreciation schedules are more accelerated than the straight-line depreciation (which would be $10,000 / 5 = $2,000 per year) that we would use for financial reporting purposes. In the following table, we give an example of an accelerated depreciation schedule (more than $2,000 is depreciated in the earlier years and less in the later years). This lowers your taxable income by more in the early years, which lowers your taxes early.

Time Period	0	1	2	3	4	5
Initial Investment	-$10,000.00					
Tax Depreciation		$3,300.00	$2,700.00	$2,000.00	$1,300.00	$700.00
Tax Shield From Depreciation @ 30%		$990.00	$810.00	$600.00	$390.00	$210.00

The present value of the tax savings (discounted at 8%) is $2,516.99. In contrast, if the tax code were to require we use straight-line depreciation, the tax savings would be deferred further into the future, and the present value would only be $2,395.63 (the present value of an annuity of 0.3 × $2,000 for five years at 8%). Certain types of investments (such as solar panels) may also qualify for special tax credits or have lower tax rates applied to them. It's best to check with your tax department to make sure you get these right.

Let's combine all the factors we've considered so far and recalculate the project's present value. As the problem starts to incorporate many factors, we'll find it clearer to use separate line items to denote the different types of cash flows.

Time Period	0	1	2	3	4	5
Initial Investment	-$10,000.00					
Pretax Savings on Electric Bill		$2,800.00	$2,940.00	$3,087.00	$3,241.35	$3,403.42
Taxes on Savings		-$840.00	-$882.00	-$926.10	-$972.41	-$1,021.03
Tax Shield from Depreciation		$990.00	$810.00	$600.00	$390.00	$210.00
Total Impact on After-tax Cash Flow	-$10,000.00	$2,950.00	$2,868.00	$2,760.90	$2,658.95	$2,592.39
Present Value of Cash Flows	-$10,000.00	$2,731.48	$2,458.85	$2,191.69	$1,954.40	$1,764.34

There are four types of cash flows: the initial investment, the tax shield from that investment (which does not occur till later), the savings on the electric bill, and the tax consequences of those savings (which happen in the same year as the savings). The total present value of the after-tax cash flows is now $1,100.76, and the project's IRR is 12.2%. The investment in solar panels is still a profitable decision.

Higher-Level Strategic Decisions

For higher-level strategic decisions such as new product introductions, opening operations in a new location, acquiring another firm, and so on, virtually every item on your income statement, cash flow statement, and balance sheet will be affected. The present-value criterion still applies, however, and the calculation techniques are exactly the same as we outlined previously; there are just more line items to forecast.

In many of these higher-level types of investment decisions there is a longer lag between when the decision to invest is made, the investment costs begin to be incurred, and the benefits start to come in. This can arise because research and development must be completed first, production facilities have to be built, regulatory approval has to be obtained, and so on. Time to market becomes an important consideration in these problems. The more quickly you can get your product to market, the more valuable the cash inflows are. Discounted cash flow techniques are a useful way to assess how much difference it makes to your profitability to adopt strategies that accelerate the time you get your product to market. Another reason why time to market is important is that the longer it takes, the greater the risk that competitors will beat you to the punch. If this happens, your cash inflows are not only received later, they're also smaller!

Firms have to continually invest to keep pace and understand that their investments often have only a short window of time to recover their investment.

Remember that present-value calculations are based on discounting future *cash flows*, not based on discounting future *accounting profits*. This is because markets for exchanging money over time trade cash, not accounting profits. Accounting profits nevertheless play an important role in the calculations. First, as we saw in the last section, they impact the calculation of one element of the cash flows: taxes. Second, it is often more natural and intuitive to initially think about a project in terms of the revenues it will generate and the production schedule that it will take to be able to satisfy these sales demands. Nevertheless, at some point in the analysis you will have to figure out when the revenues will translate into collections, and when the expenditures will be made to produce the product. Understanding the link between income and cash flow (as we discussed in chapters 1 and 2) is therefore a critical part of calculating the present value of future cash flows of a new strategy or product introduction or investment.

In fact, for projects that involve many line items, you would be wise to forecast out a complete set of financial statements: balance sheets, income statements, and cash flow statements. The discipline imposed by being forced to make all three of these statements consistent with each other over time will help make sure you get the timing of items correct. For example, projecting out a balance sheet, including both short-term assets such as receivables and inventory as well as long-term assets such as property, plant, and equipment is a good way to make sure you've properly accounted for the lead-lag relationship between earnings and cash flow, as well as between cash inflows and outflows. If your forecasts identify significant timing differences between cash inflows and outflows, this gives you an opportunity to consider alternative financing mechanisms. Making sure operational and investing plans are consistent with the other side of the balance sheet (your capital structure) is also an important way to double-check the internal consistency of all your projects.

The framework we'll use to estimate future cash flows is exactly the same as what we talked about in chapters 3 and 4. Everything starts with the project's future revenues: their level, their timing, and their growth rate. Once the revenue stream is projected, we need to estimate the expenses that will be needed to generate those revenues. This will allow us to calculate profit margins and put together an income statement. We'll also have to calculate the assets that must be obtained to provide the capacity to produce the revenues, how much lead time we must allow for before the assets are capable of generating goods and services that will lead to revenue, and so on.

Project Revenues

The single biggest driver of success is the revenues, and this is usually the most difficult part of estimating future cash flows associated with new products and strategic initiatives. This involves understanding the tastes and demands of customers, and predicting the competitive responses of other firms. Clearly, higher growth rates for revenue and growth that lasts longer can have a dramatic impact on the present value of future revenues. What factors influence how long growth lasts? As discussed previously, often it's how quickly competitors are able to launch similar or more advanced products. Nowhere is this more important to take into consideration than rapidly changing fields involving high-tech products. On the other hand, if there are significant barriers to entry, such as patent protection, the requirement of large capital expenditures, or highly specialized technical knowledge, this can significantly delay how quickly competitors can enter, and therefore increase the present value of the cash inflows.

Forecast the Future Expenses

Understanding the structure of your costs is the most important factor. Use the income statement as a guide. What will be your production, marketing, and research and development costs? How much of these are fixed costs versus variable costs? When will they be incurred? Remember that depreciation is not a cash flow, and will have to be adjusted out of the income numbers in converting them to cash flows.

Working Capital

Once we've made our initial forecasts in terms of sales and cost of sales, how do we convert these to cash inflows and outflows to perform present-value analysis? An important part of this conversion involves understanding what working capital is and why it is necessary. Working capital represents the firm's current assets and liabilities other than cash: accounts receivable, inventory, accounts payable, and so on. Cash collections lag behind sales revenue. These uncollected sales are on the balance sheet in the form of accounts receivables. Items we've bought (or built) but haven't sold yet are on the balance sheet in the form of inventory. Expenses we've recognized on the income statement but haven't paid yet are on the liability side of the balance sheet as accounts payable. We can see this in a cash flow statement in the adjustments made to reconcile net income to cash from operations.[32]

These time lags between when items are recognized on the income statement and when the cash inflows and outflows occur can be considered an investment in working capital. In calculating discounted cash flows, we must be able to predict how big these investments will be and how long until they pay off. Consider accounts receivable. The magnitude of the investment will depend on the mix of cash sales and credit sales. The length of time the investment exists depends on our collection terms, the expected credit quality of our customers, and so on. The investment in receivables is often proportional to the sales revenue, and the accounts receivable turnover ratio discussed in chapter 4 is useful in trying to make these assessments.

Similarly, the cost of goods sold number on the income statement lags behind the production of these units. The difference is our investment in inventory. The size of this investment depends on how we trade off the costs and benefits of inventory: the possibility of losing out on a sale if we're out of inventory versus the costs of holding inventory, which include the risk of obsolescence, theft, spoilage, and so on. The length of this investment depends on how long our production cycle takes and how large a buffer of inventory we wish to keep. The inventory turnover ratio we discussed in chapter 4 can provide information on how long this has taken for our other products.

Interactions with Other Projects

One of the most complex aspects of analyzing the impact of new projects on profitability is trying to anticipate the interaction (sometimes called externalities) between this project and other projects. This is challenging because there are so many potential types of interactions to consider. On the revenue side, a newly introduced product might cannibalize the revenues of other products. The question of how to time the introduction of a series of new products requires a careful balancing of the extra sales of the new product versus the sales of older product lost. On the other hand, sometimes new products will spur the sales of your other products. On the cost side, does your project involve acquiring resources that will have extra capacity that can be used to achieve side benefits on other projects, or does it put constraints on the ability of other projects to use shared resources? One of the most difficult-to-quantify externalities is the amount of *information* you learn as a result of working on your project (either about technology or about the competitive environment) that can be used to revise decisions in other areas or to help decide among other strategic alternatives in the future.

Problems in Choosing the Discount Rate

The discount rate that should be applied to the cash flows for a project is the rate the firm (and its investors) can earn on investments of equivalent risk. This is likely to be a problem handled by your finance department, but it's important to learn what policy they use and understand what its consequences are for the present value of your proposed project's cash flows. A natural starting point for an appropriate discount rate for a project is the firm's weighted average cost of capital (WACC). Recall that this is a mixture of the rates of return demanded by the firm's debt holders and shareholders. This is the rate the firm's capital suppliers expect to earn for the firm as a whole, which you can think of as the sum of all the firm's projects, broadly defined. Equivalently, it can be thought of as the appropriate discount rate for the firm's "average" project. Ideally, it should be adjusted upward or downward for each individual project, depending on how that project's risk compares to the average.

Many firms find it impractical to come up with a discount rate for every potential project, and instead group projects into categories and use a discount rate for each category. Very speculative projects, which often involve considerable research and development, untested technologies, and/or new foreign markets with unstable political or economic environments have their cash flows discounted at very high rates (say, twice the firm's WACC). Slightly less risky projects, such as developing new products, might have to earn 1.5 times the firm's WACC. Strategies that involve expanding the size of the firm should be discounted at the WACC. Safer projects, such as cost improvements that involve more familiar technology, might be discounted at lower rates, say, 0.75 times the firm's WACC.

Sometimes firms are unwilling to even make these distinctions and instead use the same discount rate for all their projects. Although this avoids having to make individual risk and discount rate decisions, this is a dangerous policy. If you use the same discount rate (or hurdle rate) for all projects, you'll make safer projects appear less valuable than they actually are (because you're discounting their cash flows at too high a rate) and make riskier projects appear more valuable. This will bias you toward a portfolio of projects whose cash flows are riskier than their expected cash flows can justify.

Other firms adjust for risk and uncertainty in other simplistic ways. The Payback Method is such a method. The Payback Method judges projects by how quickly they return their initial investment.[33] For example, the policy might be to only adopt projects that "pay back" in three years or less. Such a policy has two serious problems. The first is that simply paying back the investment ignores the opportunity cost of what the investment could have earned. If all you want is your money back, then don't invest it in the first place; keep it. To illustrate this problem, the first two examples we used in the solar panel investment decision returned their initial investment in one year and two years, respectively, yet both were poor investments because they did not earn an acceptable rate of return over and above the cost of capital. The second problem is that the Payback Method ignores any cash flows that a project will generate in time periods beyond the "threshold" or "cutoff" date, no matter how lucrative they are. For example, in our last example (with inflation and taxes), the project didn't pay back its initial investment for four years, but it was a positive present-value project because the benefits in years 4 and 5 were substantial.[34]

A second "simple" method that is better than the Payback Method is to choose projects based on their internal rate of return (IRR). The main advantage of IRR is that you can calculate a project's IRR without having to specify a discount rate. Nevertheless, you still need to establish a threshold rate of return for deciding what projects to accept; following the previous example, we would accept projects with an IRR above 8%. Moreover, this threshold should be different for riskier projects than it is for safer projects. Even holding risk aside, the project with the highest IRR is not necessarily the project with the highest present value of cash flows. Finally, although IRR is easy to calculate for projects whose cash flows have simple patterns like the ones we've talked about, it is harder (even with spreadsheets) with more complicated cash flow patterns. For example, if the cash flows start out negative, then turn positive, and then are negative at the end (due to project termination or disposal costs), the IRR is not unique. That is, there is more than one discount rate that will give the project's cash flows a total present value of zero.

Firms often intentionally make the hurdle rate they use to make internal capital allocation decisions higher than their external cost of capital. One reason they do this is to try to "offset" unrealistically high estimates of future cash flow benefits. We turn to this issue next.

Optimism, Bias, and Sensitivity Analysis

Having completed all the previous steps, we can crunch the numbers and calculate the net present value of the project's future cash flows, and our spreadsheet will give us the profitability right to the penny! This degree of exactness is of course an illusion. The numbers that come out are no more accurate than the quality of the assumptions that went into the analysis. One of the big problems you must face is that the forecasts will often be inflated because of natural optimism on the part of the people who proposed the project. It's their baby. Therefore they see only the rosiest possible outcome: it will add revenue, lead to a pathbreaking discovery, and advance the careers of the managers. The list of positive outcomes can sound too good to be true and often is. In fact, managers sometimes purposefully inflate the projections if they start to see that the present values aren't coming out as high as they hoped.

This is one of many reasons why it's valuable to step back and take a hard look at all the numbers. Redo the calculations under alternative scenarios: optimistic, pessimistic, and best-guess scenarios. To make this easier to do, it's a good idea to try to design your spreadsheet so that all the important assumptions are in the same area. This makes it easier to change them. What happens if we change the project and do it this way instead of that way? How much worse than expected does the project have to perform to lose money rather than make money? There are computer programming packages (including add-ins to popular spreadsheet programs) that can even help you map out probability distributions for profits.

The investment approval process is another important way to provide checks and balances. Bigger investments generally require higher-level approval. The largest types of investments, including corporate acquisitions, have to be approved by the board of directors. Ideally, this process is not merely rubber-stamping the ideas of managers but adds value in two ways. First, a questioning attitude can raise issues that the project's originators hadn't thought of. Second, other managers and directors will often have experience that allows them to suggest ways to improve the project.

In this chapter, we developed a framework to enable you to link your decisions and strategies directly to the economic value they create for your firm. One of the key benefits of the discounted cash flow methodology is that it does not myopically focus on short-term profits or sales; instead it is about measuring long-term economic value. This allows you to meaningfully compare strategies that differ in terms of how quickly they provide their return. Because the time value of money is the crucial economic concept underlying this technique, its success hinges on your ability to assess the timing of the inflows and outflows that will be affected by your strategic decisions. This requires the talent to lay out how your strategy will unfold in terms of transactions and events and the skills to translate these into forecasted income statements, balance sheets, and ultimately to future cash flows.

In addition to helping decide what investment decisions to pursue, these forecasted future financial statements can also provide the benchmark for assessing how well you've implemented the investment decisions you've adopted. You can then use the tools we learned in chapters 3 and 4 to analyze your performance, to reassess your strategy, and to revise it accordingly. Financial statements are important sources of information in both looking forward to invest and looking backward to assess how you've done; managers skilled in accounting and finance have an advantage at each stage of the continuing cycle of "invest, assess, and revise."

Conclusion

In this book we've introduced an important set of skills that all managers need to have in their toolkit. Managers make decisions every day that impact their firms' profits. They continually need to evaluate how their strategies have been performing and to devise new strategies to help their firms grow and improve. Accounting and finance skills enable them to understand the information that is generated about their performance, to know what additional information to collect and how to quantify the impact of their ideas into numbers, and to be able to participate in strategy discussions that involve financial effects.

We covered the vocabulary and language of accounting and finance—how business transactions and economic events get translated into the three primary financial statements, balance sheets, income statements, and cash flow statements. In addition to describing the individual elements that comprise the financial statements, we also discussed how they relate to each other. Like any new language, the quickest way to improve these newly acquired skills is to apply them and practice them. The best way to do this is with real financial statements. Public companies' financial statements are embedded in their annual reports, which they make available to shareholders, and their Form 10-K, which they file with the Securities and Exchange Commission. Find a copy of your own company's annual report and read through it.[35] Not only will this be a chance to apply your new knowledge of finance and accounting, but you'll also learn a lot about your company.

Start by skimming through it just to see what it looks like. You might be surprised at how long it is. The annual report generally starts with a long section in which the company describes itself and its products, and highlights its performance. This material is largely unaudited; companies have a lot of discretion to decide what to talk about and what to downplay or even exclude. For example, if they did well in a customer satisfaction survey they can highlight this, if they didn't, they won't mention the topic at all. Next come the financial statements themselves. Finally, there are many dozens of pages of footnotes. The footnotes provide supporting information and details and the assumptions that underlie the financial statements.

Once you've skimmed the report as a whole, let's go straight to the financial statements. Most of it should look familiar, although there will be some line items that are new. Don't be alarmed by this; you'll be able to pick up more and more of the information each time you go back and look at it. Now let's do some of the calculations we covered in chapters 3 and 4. Start with the income statement. What were revenues and how much did they grow? Did the company make a profit? Calculate the profit margins and look at which costs ate up the most revenues. Were there any "one-time" items that had a big impact on profits? Now compare last year to the year before. Look at the balance sheet and see if the composition of the assets has changed much from last year to this year. Calculate the company's return on assets and return on equity. Which is higher, and how does that relate to the company's leverage? How much debt does the company have? Has its capital structure changed much? What were the company's primary sources and uses of cash? Is the company investing a lot for the future? How much did they pay out in dividends?

Having done this, go back to the first part of the annual report. Find the section titled "Management Discussion and Analysis." Here the company will provide a more complete discussion of its performance and compare this year's performance to last years. How does what they say compare to what you discovered when you went through the financial statements yourself? What else did the company talk about? Note that there is a section on risk factors the company faces and a section about critical accounting policies, in which the company describes the accounting policies that require the most judgment and make the biggest impact on the financial statements.

Finally, go to the footnote section. Because these are so densely written, many readers skip them. Don't make this mistake; these contain a lot of useful information. Take your time, and pick out a few at a time and go through them. If there are new terms, try to find their definitions. If the company doesn't define them somewhere in the annual report, the Internet is a good place to look up financial terminology. See if the company provides information in the footnotes about how its individual segments performed. Having gone through your company's annual report, do the same thing for a competitor's financial statements. How do you compare?

Another easy way to apply your new knowledge is by reading the business press. Newspapers, business magazines, and the Internet include articles every day in which companies' finance and accounting issues play a major role. Try to read a few of these on a regular basis. Again, you'll find that the more you do this, the more you'll pick up, and the easier the next article will be to read.

It's harder to use public financial statements to practice discounted cash flow techniques, but there are other ways to do this. Get a computer spreadsheet program (such as Excel) and practice with the present-value functions like PV (for annuities) and NPV (for more general cash flow streams). See if you can replicate the discounted cash flow examples we did in the chapter. Then apply discounted cash flow techniques to some personal finance situations. If you have an automobile loan or mortgage on a house, see if you can verify your monthly payment. Then construct an amortization schedule to see how the loan gets paid off. If you have children who will be going off to college, try to calculate how much you have to begin putting aside per year to be able to pay their college costs. Try doing the same thing to see how much to start saving if you want to have accumulated a nest egg for when you retire.

Most important, start using this knowledge on the job. Once you become comfortable with the vocabulary, use it in discussions with colleagues and ask questions of the people in accounting and finance. Although this ebook has introduced many important issues, there are plenty of textbooks that can help you broaden and deepen your newfound skills. Take advantage of them! The more you know about financial issues, the better equipped you will be to oversee your firm's operations, use your resources more efficiently, and boost revenues and profits. That's the bottom line.

Acknowledgments

I would like to thank Peter Knutson, who started the finance and accounting executive education program at Wharton. Peter gave me the opportunity to begin teaching in the program early in my career as a professor, generously shared his teaching materials he developed over the years, and groomed me to take over the program when he retired. I would also like to thank Professors Brian Bushee, Ro Verrecchia, Bob Holthausen, and Chris Ittner, all fabulous teachers who have been great colleagues and mainstays in the program for many years. Finally, I would like to thank Gary Stern and Shannon Berning for their expert assistance in writing this book and keeping me on schedule.

Appendix

More on the Cash Flow Statement: The Indirect Method

Companies generally present their cash flow statement using the indirect method, so if you want to be able to read and interpret a "real" cash flow statement, you need to understand the material in this appendix. In addition, these techniques are helpful in learning how to convert from income numbers to cash flows, which is an important skill in performing discounted cash flow analysis.

I'll first present what the Operating Section would look like under the Indirect Method, then we'll talk through it.

Accent Inc.
Statement of Cash Flows—Indirect Method
(Operating Section Only)

Operating Activities	
Net Income	$2,850
Add: Depreciation	$4,000
Less: Increase in Accounts Receivable	($17,000)
Increase in Inventory	($20,000)
Add: Increase in Accounts Payable	$23,000
Increase in Taxes Payable	$1,900
Increase in Compensation Payable	$1,000
Increase in Interest Payable	$250
Cash from Operations	($4,000)

This yields the same total for cash from operations as we saw in the example at the end of chapter 2, but it looks very different. Most readers other than experienced analysts find this fairly confusing rather than illuminating. Nevertheless, unless accounting standard setters force companies to present using the Direct Method detailed in the text (for which there is growing support), companies will continue to report using the Indirect Method. Therefore, it's useful to know how these adjustments work.

The starting point is Net Income, which involves revenues minus expenses. Because not all of these are in the form of cash, we adjust out the noncash portion. To figure out the noncash portion, we look to the balance sheet (more specifically, the change in the balance sheet).

For the revenue line in the income statement, the part of revenue that isn't cash went into the receivables asset on the balance sheet. For Accent Inc., receivables went up by $16,000 during the year (it started at zero), which means cash received was lower by $16,000 than the sales recorded. This means we have to lower the Net Income number by $16,000 to convert from income to cash. We have to make similar adjustments for the other items. Not all of the compensation expense was paid in cash; the noncash portion is in the wages payable liability account on the balance sheet. Because the cash outflow wasn't as big as the expense we recorded, we have to make a positive adjustment to Net Income. Similar adjustments are made for the interest expense not being paid yet (which shows up in the Notes Payable account), the tax expense not being paid yet (which shows up in the Taxes Payable account), and the depreciation expense (which shows up as a reduction in the Property, Plant, and Equipment asset account). The most complicated adjustment is for Cost of Goods Sold on the income statement. In this case, we need to make two adjustments. First, we bought more units than we sold, which would make the cash outlay bigger than the expense recorded in the income statement, other things equal. This requires a negative adjustment, and it reflects the increase in the Inventory Account. Second, we didn't pay for all the purchases in cash, which works in the other direction. This is a positive adjustment, and it reflects the increase in Accounts Payable of $23,000.

Because all the beginning balances are zeros, all the asset and liability accounts increased. As we see from the sign of the adjustments, increases in assets use up cash, and increases in liabilities generate (or save) cash. Although we don't have any in our example, decreases in balance sheet accounts work in exactly the opposite way. A decrease in an asset results in a positive adjustment (the benefit has been received), and a decrease in a liability results in a negative adjustment (the liability is paid off). One of the most frequently misunderstood adjustments on the statement is the "add-back" for depreciation. This is frequently (mis)interpreted as the amount of cash that was provided by depreciation. Depreciation does not add cash. The adjustment is there merely to offset the fact that depreciation expense appears as a subtraction in the calculation of net income. If we had more depreciation, there would be a bigger add-back for depreciation on the cash flow statement, but the net income would also have been lower. These two things always offset each other; depreciation is not a cash flow, so its net effect on the cash flow statement is zero.

Endnotes

1 In the United States, public companies have to file reports quarterly with the Securities and Exchange Commission (SEC) using accounting rules called Generally Accepted Accounting Principles (GAAP). These rules are established by a private-sector body called the Financial Accounting Standards Board (FASB). Internationally, many companies use International Financial Reporting Standards (IFRS), which are established by the International Accounting Standards Board (IASB), headquartered in London. Some countries (similar to the United States) have their own standards. Moreover, all firms—both public and private—have to file tax returns, which require compiling financial information using the rules specified in the tax code.

2 On the other hand, for many complicated financial instruments like derivatives, there is not an easily determined market price, and fair values have to be estimated using complex (and often subjective) valuation models. Even when market prices are available, this does not necessarily represent the best estimate of the asset's long-term value. In particular, when the only observed trades are by firms in deep financial distress, as happened during the recent liquidity crisis and market meltdown, the "fire sale" prices that are observed are not reflective of what similar-looking assets are worth for firms who can ride out the crisis.

3 In principle, brand values could certainly be estimated by independent valuation experts. For example, the brand valuation consulting firm Interbrand estimated that the brand value of Coke was $70 billion during 2010. However, current accounting rules deem these values to be too "soft" or imprecise to put onto the financial statements.

4 For example, research and development and advertising costs are generally expensed (and not treated as assets) under U.S. GAAP, yet in some industries this is their major form of investment and the major expenditure they make to try to generate future benefits.

5 When a firm makes an acquisition, they have to allocate the purchase price to all the individual assets and liabilities they have obtained. Any amount that cannot be attributed to something else is classified as goodwill on the acquiring firm's balance sheet.

6 As noted in this section, there is sometimes controversy regarding which section of the cash flow statement an item should appear in. Moreover, whereas is difficult to manipulate the cash given the transactions and events that occurred, it is easy to design transactions to impact when the cash flows occur. For example, consider the choice between giving workers a wage increase versus increasing their pension benefits. Even if these are designed to have exactly the same economic cost (in present-value terms), their impact on (the timing of) cash is extremely different. This is one of the reasons why many government bodies, who tend to administer their budgets on a cash basis, are in the dire financial situation they're in now. They approved generous pension benefits for their workers, put little or no money aside to cover these benefits, and therefore didn't have to worry about those costs in their cash-based budgets while they were in office. Now, years later, the pension benefits are due and there's no money to pay for them.

7 For example, for many years, Microsoft has been criticized for the huge war chest of cash and short-term investments they keep on hand. Similar questions are being raised about the amount of cash Apple is keeping.

8 There are many measures of performance that are overhyped by consulting firms and others as "the" measure to look at. Business performance is complicated and multidimensional; it's always a good idea to check to see exactly what a given measure incorporates and what it leaves out.

9 One of the challenges here is finding detailed data on other firms. Public firms must file financial statements with the SEC (or similar agencies in other countries); however, private firms have no obligation to do so. Several websites provide information about financial ratios for industries, sectors of the economy, and the S&P 500 as a whole, but these sources are also subject to the limitations of using publicly available data.

10 Growth is commonly measured using sales revenue, but a growth rate can be calculated for any variable, such as profits, assets, number of stores, and so on, by simply calculating the percentage change in that variable over time:

$$\frac{\text{Current period amount} - \text{prior period amount}}{\text{prior period amount}}$$

Note: It doesn't make sense to calculate growth off of a negative base, and growth cannot be calculated if the prior period amount is zero. These kinds of results cannot happen with sales, but they can happen when calculating earnings growth (because earnings can be negative).

11 Simon, B., (February 24, 2010), "Japan PM Seeks to Defuse Toyota Friction," *Financial Times*.

12 Like most companies, PepsiCo does not publicly disclose a full income statement for each of its segments, so our calculations are based on the numbers they provide. As discussed later in this section, operating profit does not include interest expense or income taxes, so keep that in mind in evaluating the magnitude of the margins.

13 One real economic difference between LIFO and FIFO firms relates to taxes. LIFO reports lower income when costs are rising; FIFO reports lower income when costs are falling. Therefore, if a firm wanted to reduce its taxes, firms in industries where costs are rising should use LIFO, and firms in industries where costs are falling (e.g., many high-tech industries) would use FIFO. However, there is a catch to this. This is one of the few situations where your choice has to be the same on your tax return as it is on your reports to shareholders. Therefore, if a firm chooses LIFO to lower its taxes, it will also be reporting lower income to shareholders. Companies therefore have to choose which is more important to them: reporting higher accounting profits to shareholders or saving real dollars in taxes. A surprisingly large number of firms choose the former, apparently believing that investors and creditors are not sophisticated enough to understand that this is what is making their earnings higher. There is enough disclosure required in the firm's footnotes regarding this issue to enable investors and creditors to see through this, and empirical evidence suggests that they do make these adjustments when valuing a firm.

14 Consistent with this, empirical evidence suggests that firms whose CEOs are near retirement age tend to conduct less R&D.

15 Shankland, S., (January 16, 2003), "Sun Charges Lead to $2.3 Billion Loss," CNET News.

16 Krisher, T., (November 7, 2007), "GM Posts Whopping $39B Loss for 3Q Due to Charges, 2nd Biggest Quarterly Loss Ever," Associated Press.

17 In doing this, we have to be careful because interest expense is tax deductible, and the net income number is after tax. Suppose a firm earned a net income of $1,035 and it paid $100 of interest expense. Obviously, the interest lowered pretax income by $100, but it also lowered taxes by $35 (assuming a 35% tax rate). The after-tax impact of the interest expense is therefore only $65, or (1 – tax rate) × interest expense. The firm's income before interest is therefore $1,035 + $65 = $1,100.

18 Even for an investment of zero risk, investors (whether debt holders or equity holders) will want a return that at least compensates them for expected inflation. This base rate of return has historically been the U.S. Treasury bill rate, although political developments in the summer of 2011 have led people to begin to question whether there is a risk of default even in U.S. government-backed securities. Investors then add a premium to this base rate to compensate them for bearing risk.

19 When debt holders loan money to a firm, they are promised a prespecified interest rate (say, 5%). No matter how spectacularly the borrower performs, it's not going to pay the lender more interest than the loan stipulates. The lender's return is therefore capped from above. However, there is a chance the borrower will default and the lender will receive less than the stated interest rate (in the extreme he receives zero). This means that the lender's expected rate of return will be less than the promised 5% if there is a probability of default. The greater the probability of default, the lower the lender's expected rate of return would be. In order to be willing to lend money to risky borrowers yet still earn an acceptable expected rate of return, the lender has to charge a higher interest rate (that is only paid when the borrower turns out to be solvent) to offset the loss the lender bears in the event the borrower defaults. Therefore, the cost of debt to a firm is directly related to the riskiness of the firm's cash flows and the probability of defaulting on the loan. There are ratings agencies such as Moody's, Standard & Poor's, and Fitch's, who specialize in analyzing debt securities and classifying them according to their riskiness.

20 This is an additional motivation for comparing ratios to the past or to competitors. If the accounting biases are stable over time or similar across firms, the relative comparisons will wash them out and allow us to see any real improvements.

21 Finance experts have a way of measuring this sensitivity to overall market movements; it's called your beta coefficient. If the market as whole (say, the S&P 500 index) moves up or down by 1%, a firm with a beta of 1.0 would also tend to move by 1% (and in the same direction), whereas a firm with a beta of 2.0 would tend to move twice as much, and a firm with a beta of 0.5 would only move half as much. The bigger your beta, the more sensitive your profits are to overall market movements, and the riskier you are viewed to be. Accordingly, shareholders in high-beta firms demand a high rate of return to compensate them for this risk. The cost of equity capital for a firm is then equal to the risk free rate (that is, the rate on Treasury bills) plus a premium for the firm's market-related risk. The market as a whole, which has a beta of 1.0, has historically yielded a premium of approximately 5% greater than the risk-free rate. A firm with a beta of 0.5 would require a premium of half this, or 2.5% over the risk-free rate, and so on.

22 Rogers, C., (May 20, 2011), "GM Creating Low Cost, Eco-Friendly Production," *The Detroit News.*

23 Estimating which costs are fixed and which are variable is based on a combination of judgment and experience in observing how the costs behave, as well as statistical techniques that provide estimates of the fixed and variable portions of costs. Regression analysis, which attempts to fit the best straight line that explains the relationship between costs and, say, production volume, is a common example.

24 Howell, D., (June 14, 2011), "Google to Help Bring Solar to 8,000 or More Homes Unusual $280 Mil Investment Creates Fund SolarCity Will Use to Install Systems That It Leases to Owners Long Term," *Investor's Business Daily.*

25 A period of time can be however long as suits the problem you're interested in analyzing. The most common lengths are monthly or annual periods. You have to be careful to make sure your interest (or discount) rate is consistent with your length of a period. That is, if a period of time is a year, the discount rate has to be an annual rate of return; if a period is one month, the discount rate has to be a monthly rate of return.

26 We'd see this if we had borrowed $10,000 to finance this investment. If the lender charges 8% interest (his opportunity cost for investments of similar risk), our interest expense would be $800. Now our $10,500 savings are not enough to pay off this interest and the principal balance of the loan of $10,000. However, if we'd financed the investment with equity (either by issuing shares or out of retained earnings), no charge for the use of this capital would show up on our income statement. Nevertheless, it's not free! The cost is the opportunity to use the money elsewhere and earn 8%.

27 This is exactly analogous to the following choice: which would you rather be given, a brand-new Rolls Royce or a bicycle? Even if you don't know how to drive a car, you should take the Rolls Royce because you can sell it, buy the bicycle you want, and have money left over.

28 Annuities are extremely common cash flow patterns, not only in investment projects, but also in many financial contracts, including mortgages and bonds.

29 You should always check the instructions of your calculator or spreadsheet to verify the type of input it is expecting. For example, is an 8% interest rate input as an 8 or as 0.08? Is a positive number for a cash flow considered an inflow or an outflow? The Excel PV function, for example, will return an answer of negative $11,979.59 if you ask it to calculate the PV of an annuity of $2,800 a year for five years at 8%. If you want the answer to be positive because this is part of some bigger calculation, you have to change it on your own.

30 If the discount rate we used to calculate the present value of future cash is a market rate of interest, it has a premium for expected inflation built into it. We therefore also need expectations regarding inflation to be built into the cash flow estimates to make them consistent with the discount rate.

31 In Excel the function is called NPV. This function presumes that the first cash flow in the pattern occurs one period from now. If you've got a cash flow that occurs at the present time (like our initial cash outlay), you can't include it as part of the Excel NPV function's calculation. Instead, you have to add it in separately to calculate the total present value.

32 For example, we can express the relation between collections, sales, and receivables as:

Cash Collected = Sales – Change in Accounts Receivable

An increase in receivables means that cash collected is less than the sales revenue. We can think of the extra sales revenue as being invested in the receivables rather than being collected immediately.

33 You often see this same "logic" used in mortgage refinancing advice: look at how much it costs to refinance and divide this by the change in your monthly payments. This is how long it takes you to "recoup" your refinancing costs. While this is a good start to the analysis, the problem with this logic is that it ignores the fact that you could have invested that money somewhere else and earned a return. If this return is bigger than your mortgage savings, refinancing is probably not a good idea.

34 Although the Payback Method seems like it avoids having to specify the interest rate that should be used for a project, it does this by implicitly assuming a very unrealistic set of interest rates: an interest rate of zero up through the cutoff date and an interest rate of infinity beyond this. Needless to say, this is a dramatic and unrealistic set of interest rates!

35 If it's a public company, there should be a copy in the investor relations section of your company's website. If not, get a copy from within the company itself.

Index

About the Author

Richard A. Lambert is Miller-Sherrerd Professor of Accounting at the Wharton School of the University of Pennsylvania, where he teaches finance and accounting in the MBA and Executive Education programs, as well as seminars in the doctoral program. The recipient of several teaching awards, his articles have appeared in *The Accounting Review, Journal of Accounting Research, Journal of Accounting and Economics, Rand Journal of Economics,* and *Strategic Management Journal.*

About Wharton Digital Press

Wharton Digital Press was established to inspire bold, insightful thinking within the global business community. In the tradition of The Wharton School of the University of Pennsylvania and its online business journal *Knowledge@Wharton*, Wharton Digital Press uses innovative digital technologies to help managers meet the challenges of today and tomorrow.

As an entrepreneurial publisher, Wharton Digital Press delivers relevant, accessible, conceptually sound, and empirically based business knowledge to readers wherever and whenever they need it. Its format ranges from ebooks and enhanced ebooks to mobile apps and print books available through print-on-demand technology. Directed to a general business audience, the Press's areas of interest include management and strategy, innovation and entrepreneurship, finance and investment, leadership, marketing, operations, human resources, social responsibility, business-government relations, and more.

http://wdp.wharton.upenn.edu

Wharton
UNIVERSITY *of* PENNSYLVANIA

About The Wharton School

The Wharton School of the University of Pennsylvania—founded in 1881 as the first collegiate business school—is recognized globally for intellectual leadership and ongoing innovation across every major discipline of business education. The most comprehensive source of business knowledge in the world, Wharton bridges research and practice through its broad engagement with the global business community. The School has more than 4,800 undergraduate, MBA, executive MBA, and doctoral students; more than 9,000 annual participants in executive education programs; and an alumni network of 86,000 graduates.

http://www.wharton.upenn.edu